DEBORAH HOLMÉN

IT TAKES A LOT OF Sh*t TO GROW BEAUTIFUL FLOWERS

A Gardener's Guide to Life

Book Cover by Deborah Holmén, Canva Pro

Illustrations by Atticus

First edition 2024

Contents

Prologue

DISCLAIMER: This isn't a story about dysfunctional families suffering from drug or alcohol abuse, although our mother pushed copious amounts of Cod Liver Oil and Vitamin C down our throats, which should have been considered illegal. At a young age, I believed that if I had taken illicit drugs, I would have died immediately without feeling the high, ecstasy, or whatever it is people feel when they want to escape into the ether.

My body revolted against me at age 15, so I decided from that point on drugs -of any kind- would be my demise. I figured my body wanted peace from the years of infliction my mother and sister caused me at such a young age. My body was probably ready to check out without much assistance.

I, however, wasn't ready to leave so soon. I was fifteen when my lung collapsed. All the bicycling I was doing back and forth to work at my parent's nursery and florist shop, a twenty-five-mile round trip, caused me to lose a lot of body fat. I was always slender, but I had no idea something so healthy as exercising could push my body to revolt.

I was born with thin spots, or blebs, on the lobes of my lung. What little layer of fat in my body kept them from bursting until I had done too much. So, as the doctors told me later, I was thin, muscular, and healthy, but I had inadequate fat to protect my lung from collapsing when a bleb popped. The doctors left me with 60% of my right lung and an appreciation for structural medicine.

I spent six long weeks in the hospital flirting with a boy I liked in high school, and he eventually invited me to prom. Yes, I had my priorities, even with ten feet of tubing oozing bodily fluids out of my side.

He was my respite, giving me something to be hopeful about. He was also my refuge from the onslaught of insults and belittling from my sister and the judgment and condemnation from my mother. I spent every waking moment at his family's home after school for four years.

I am extremely humbled that my experiences were of a distinctively different dysfunctional nature. This isn't to say this book will be a trip through the tulips, either. All of us have stories to share, and in our stories, we reveal the path our Soul is meant to be on, no matter how painful and traumatizing it can be.

My hero complex toward my parents disintegrated at a very young age. I saw my parents for who they were, realizing they had their own stuff to go through, and I was merely a witness to it all. This made me a survivor, determined I would be much healthier once I was out of their care.

So, at nineteen, I filed for Independence from my parents and moved out to a friend's home for the summer. I planned to attend college out of state and was accepted into Roanoke College with financial aid and a job waiting for me. Things were looking up.

I think back to that summer, wondering what my life would be like if I had taken that route to Roanoke. After being gone for the summer, my parents promised to make amends and paid for me to attend the University of Maryland, College Park, that fall. They were putting my brother and older sister through college, so their guilt may have brought me back into the fold.

This is also not a story about mental disorders; however, that would have helped me understand the symptoms of my family's dysfunction much easier if there was an apparent mental disorder to blame - some family legacy of why my parents and sister behaved the way they did toward me.

If they were alcoholics or addicts, it would have seemed more plausible than a staunch religious belief, birth order, or a need for control. I'm not aware of any well-known survivor with a traumatic past rising from the ashes due to sibling abuse or a parent's staunch Catholic creed. Then again, any type of dissonance in a child's life can impact them for years.

If you may suffer from diagnosed or undiagnosed psychological issues, work with a certified professional for proper treatment. I say this since I have befriended many over the years who had psychological issues, and without the proper treatment protocols, their conditions worsened.

In our lives, the tapestry of our experiences is shaped by the threads of memory. But how reliable are these threads? This question urges us to reconsider our understanding of memory and its relationship to truth.

I believe that memory holds its own truth, but it requires us to broaden our understanding of its complexities. I've come to realize that authenticity doesn't stem from a clear distinction between fact and fiction but rather from the intricate interplay of memory and imagination.

When I look back on my own life, I understand that my memories are deeply personal and uniquely mine. Instead of seeking absolute truths from others, I acknowledge the subjective nature of these memories, recognizing how they are shaped by my perceptions, emotions, and the context of my life at that time.

Through this exploration, I've come to a profound realization: the past is not a fixed entity but rather a tapestry woven from my interpretations and the inherent mysteries of memory. Embracing this complexity allows me to approach my past with greater empathy and understanding, acknowledging that each person's perspective is shaped by their own unique journey.

This is more or less a story, totally based on my experiences as a very young girl in a dysfunctional family and how I overcame the *shit* I went through to grow into a decent human being. Manure and dung may seem unpleasant and unnecessary, but they ultimately provide essential nutrients for plants and flowers to grow. The challenges and setbacks I faced were catalysts for my personal growth.

Ironically, the word 'shit' makes me cringe. I never used curse words to emphasize my meaning or stance on things- there are better words to describe a person's feelings than profanity. However, I realized that when talking to many trauma survivors, this term was used frequently. It was like it represented the worst situation, feeling, or moment that summed it all up, and only those types of words fit precisely and said it all.

Years later, I learned from a sage young man that my lung experience was one of my 'exit points.' He shared his beliefs that we have many exit points to check out from a difficult life, and I was grateful that I didn't choose to leave this beautiful blue ball at the time of my collapsed lung. He said I had several "exit points" since my upbringing had caused me much pain and trauma.

It did. I won't deny that, but I knew I was meant for more. I felt I was here to learn something so that my Soul could grow. Those foundational years with my problemed family taught me a lot about the human condition, how we put expectations on those we love, and how those expectations can harm our well-being.

I don't regret the things I experienced. I look at them now, similar to cultivating rough and barren soil by using a lot of rich manure to make a beautiful garden and grow brilliant flowers.

If you have ever created a garden, you would realize a lot of toil and sweat goes into the foundation of the soil. You must remove the weeds and top grassy sod, then sift through the soil underneath to expose rocks, roots, and whatnot.

This is where it all begins, at the most naked and revealing place. We all have this bare soil within us; getting to its source and uncovering its true potential is the first and most challenging step.

However, some want to avoid looking under the surface to reveal what may be lurking in their dirt. They will cover it with pretty petals of clothes, cars, and finer things. They might stay in the mire of drugs, deception, and self-hate. They smooth out any lumps and bumps with a story they tell themselves and convince others to repeat it. The storytelling becomes like a Virginia creeper vine whose roots meander to all near enough to hear, growing more of the lie.

But what happens to our souls when the story we tell ourselves is like this evasive weed? Will we eventually choke on our lies and deception?

The good news is you can prune and dismantle that vine of lies and start fresh by tilling and cultivating a new you. It has been proven over and over that our brain is a flexible and malleable organ that can grow new synapses and connections. So can you, if you decide you want that change.

Then, it's a matter of putting nutrients and fertilizers back into the soil, giving the seeds of promise in your life a chance to thrive.

The fertilizer represents our experiences. These experiences are there to teach us, and what we learn from them helps enrich our soil and builds the character of our soul.

As many know, these teachable moments usually cause pain and discomfort. The "manure" or fertilizers are the people we meet on our journeys, like family members, friends, colleagues, and people we have chance encounters. It could be a new job, unexpected health conditions, infidelity, or betrayal in a relationship. The examples are numerous.

These fertile experiences help us develop our character by overcoming adversity, learning from failure, handling disappointment, and developing resilience. Notice that most fertilizer that helps us grow is through pain, trauma, and hardships- or the *shit* we must endure to learn.

Sometimes, however, the fertilizers are too much, too strong, and overpowering, causing us to wither and die. Abusive relationships, substance abuse, and dysfunctional parenting can expose our garden to toxins where seemingly nothing positive will grow. This is where the challenge occurs. At this point, we must choose to uproot what we have created, move to a new plot of earth, and try again. This may be nothing more than stepping away from a volatile family member, getting divorced, moving to a new home, changing jobs, releasing toxic friendships, finding a new medical approach, etc.

At this point, we must add the crucial nutrients our gardens may be craving. These nutrients take our barren soil and enrich it with love. This could be self-care, counseling, taking classes, joining a community group, or attending a religious or spiritual center. All these nutrients add beneficial ingredients to rebuild our soil and create the perfect foundation for our garden.

Then, what comes from these challenging efforts will create an abundance of flowers. New relationships will blossom, a new job may be offered, a conflict may be resolved, and many other things can bloom from putting in the effort to change your soil.

This path may sound all rosy, but most of us know that the biggest challenge is taking the first step to recognize what is not working for us and making the change.

We till the soil, weed, water, and wait. Sometimes, the weather wreaks havoc, or the seed is not meant to take hold and grow. We must see this with a new set of eyes when this occurs.

When things fail to grow in your life, it may be that they weren't meant to grow in the first place. A friendship might have run its course due to the lessons that needed to be learned. The failed marriage may have taught you many lessons about yourself and your partner; now it's time to move on. A job may have become stagnant or unhealthy.

Sometimes, you play a part in someone else's journey. You may have been the pawn in their story, and your presence in their life helped them learn an important lesson. You were their mirror, showing them what they needed to learn.

Creating our garden connects us to the most intimate part of ourselves. We must accept the cycle of life: birth, growth, development, and death. Assuming that you did all you could, letting it return to the earth from where it came allows you to accept things as they are—a journey of hope, life experiences, and lessons.

Some of us have an innate ability to grow our gardens. They thrive regardless of what comes their way. They plant a seed of desire and watch it sprout and bloom. They cultivate and produce more, and they experience the fullness of their efforts. They are directly connected to Mother Nature—the source of all that makes things grow. You may have another name for this energy that causes the ebbs and flows of Life — the ultimate Source of all things. Regardless of its name, it is there for all of us to use.

Others find themselves moving from one plot of land to another, keeping their gardening techniques the same with each move. They wonder why their seeds still won't grow into something beautiful. The soil is neglected, the seeds are thrown in, and they hope it will be different this time. Still, the ravages of this uncultivated approach to their life will always give them the same harvest of regret, fear, and frustration.

We are all meant to live rich and fulfilling lives and develop into the people we will become. Many are born without a nurturing foundation to lean on when times are tough. They might have been given guardians who neglected, abused, or didn't want them. These souls grow up with weaker roots because they don't see themselves as whole people but as broken, wilted, or infested with behaviors taught to them.

This doesn't mean they should be cast off to the compost heap. It means they need to be given a chance to reroot in better soil and prune out their old and tired beliefs, providing a chance for a new beginning. These propagated people may stay stunted, but at least they are given another opportunity to grow and flourish.

Regardless of the garden you came from, it doesn't mean you can't find a new plot of land and till the earth, until it's raw and naked, and begin again. We all carry an original seed whose chaff is ready to receive sunlight to split open and grow.

Plant yourself into that newly freshened soil, feed it only the best fertilizers, and love. Give it time, Sun, and water to wash away the old growth. Witness new growth unfold in your life, and your garden will flourish under your care.

It all starts by planting a seed of desire and the courage to start again. Let's begin using what gardeners and farmers know about the lessons Mother Nature can teach us. Don't be surprised if you have an urge to create a plot of earth to grow your own.

Tilth:

The general health of the soil includes a balance of nutrients, water, and air. Eliminating weeds and preparing the soil for your flowers and vegetables are important first steps in preparing a new garden. Soil that is healthy and has good physical qualities is in good tilth.

CHAPTER ONE

The Family Garden:

IDENTIFYING THE GOOD AND BAD TILTH IN YOUR GARDEN

My high school boyfriend's parents peered through the living room window, watching my Mom park the car. I sat in the kitchen with their son, Shawn. We had the same point of view from the kitchen to the front porch door. We watched Mom wobble around the car and storm up the front walkway. I could see her face, her mouth twisted in anger. I stood up from the kitchen table next to Shawn, who was protecting me like a guard dog.

To everyone's shock, she opened the glass porch door and stormed into the house. No knock, no doorbell ring. She just barged inside. MaryBelle and Bill Teter stood silent, shocked that my mother's fury invaded their tranquil home.

MaryBelle, her hair in curlers and dressed in her navy floral housecoat, shrieked and ran into the kitchen through the dining room as my mom walked straight toward me.

Bill followed, reaching for his gray jogging sweatshirt and slowly zipped it up. He assessed the situation with his gentle smile, "Now... now...now... Mrs. Chapman. What can we do for you?"

They both stood behind Shawn and me, dumbfounded that this strange woman forced herself into their house unannounced.

My heartbeat surged into the veins in my neck where surely everyone could see it pulsating. I thought at that moment how a heart attack must feel and wished one upon myself to distract everyone from this mortifying scene. My dying might shock my mother to her senses.

Shawn's voice was calm yet shaking. "Mrs. Chapman is there something I can help you with?" he asked, pulling me tighter behind him. He looked at his parents' faces and stepped forward.

It was an odd question, like something a checker would ask in the grocery store. I figured he was running on adrenaline like me, and his mind was shorting out. I almost laughed, which seemed so out of place for the situation. Maybe it was the absurdity of watching my portly Mom take such a cruel stance against me, showing the world how crazy my life had become.

"Don't you dare tell me what to do, Shawn! Calm down, my foot!" my mother screamed, shaking her finger in his face. Shawn stifled a chuckle at the archaic term. I hit his hand so as not to provoke her more. She said his name with such disdain. At that point, she reached over his arm and lunged at my neck.

I stepped back, unsure how far she would take this. She grabbed my new necklace, yanked it off me, and reached for Shawn's matching necklace. Luckily, she missed her mark as he turned away from her.

MaryBelle pulled me into her, and hot tears rolled down my cheeks. I looked at this bizarre woman before me, shaking my gold half-heart necklace at us. Bill walked around the table between my mother and his son.

My mother ignored his proximity. "You two are carrying on like you two are married!" my mother yelled, shaking her hand at Shawn and me. Tiny beads of sweat had formed on her fuzz-laden upper lip. "Enough of this!" she said, waving her arms as if to cast a spell to end us.

She then turned to MaryBelle and Bill, pointing at them. "And you two! You allow this in your own home?"

Bill spoke, almost chuckling at the absurdity of the intrusion. "Now, Mrs. Chapman, we love your daughter very much and consider her a part of our family. We could talk about this civilly if you could just sit down."

I knew Bill's calming demeanor would only enrage her more, and it did. My mother's voice hit a shrill, only heard when she yelled at my father. Her face reddened, and her hands visibly shaking.

"I forbid these two from seeing each other anymore, and I expect you two to respect my and her father's wishes!"

I had to look down at this point. I felt ashamed that my family's dysfunction was now out for all to see. MaryBelle and Bill had heard from Shawn about my mother's craziness over the four years we'd been dating. They knew of her desire to keep me from dating anyone, and they never allowed Shawn in our home since it would mean they accepted our relationship. Now, the Teters were witnessing it firsthand.

It was odd when she mentioned my father. I wondered what my dad was thinking then and realized he wasn't there supporting her. Maybe it was his way of showing her that her restrictive and judgmental beliefs had gone too far against his daughter.

Oddly, my mother and father had never met the Teter family throughout those four years. The simple fact that the Teter family wasn't Catholic was enough to entrench them into non-existence. In my mother's mind, they were heathens. Her daughter was meant to become a Nun in the Church, so keeping me chaste was the only way I'd be accepted into the Sisterhood.

I felt like I had been dropped into the 1800s, an era when women weren't supposed to have desires or dreams of independence and adventure. It was 1987, and no one understood the isolation I had felt growing up with a mother who saw her three children as a means to an end. Children were what good Catholics were to have, from a list of other dogmas they must follow to get into Heaven.

My older sister Sable made it known that she didn't believe in such a restrictive religion. I wasn't so staunch on my feelings toward religion. It had good merits, guiding people with set rules to follow and direction toward a better life. I didn't knock people who wanted comfort in times of strife. But it was my mother's extreme judgment against those of other religions that made it almost impossible to convince her that the Teter family was upstanding in the community.

MaryBelle stepped before Shawn like a mother bear protecting her cub, standing over my mother.

"Mrs. Chapman, it is best you leave my home and settle yourself down. We can talk about this when you're calm. But as far as my son and your daughter dating, they have proven to be a very responsible and loving couple. They are almost twenty and can now make their own choices. Besides, even the President of Debbie's university agrees she is free to date as she has proven herself to be a mature and responsible young lady."

My mother's face twisted as if Mary were speaking a foreign language. I had forgotten the embarrassment my mother caused me during my freshman year when she called the president of my college and told him to cloister me on campus, not allowing me to leave on the weekends to see Shawn.

To be called into the grand administration building as a freshman was terrifying, but the meeting went surprisingly well. He told me my grades and responsibilities were being met and that being eighteen meant I was independent to do as I please. There was a God! Point for Debbie, zero for Mom.

Trying to reason with my mother was like throwing oil on a fire. She didn't even acknowledge Mary's retort. My mother's voice boomed, "I don't know what religion you people are, but you surely aren't following God's book!"

Bill looked at his wife, "Now, June, I think it's time you leave," he said sternly, putting his hands out and guiding her to the door.

My mother's jaw clenched, and she threw my broken necklace at me. I picked it up and did not move to leave. I couldn't. I knew that if I went with her, I would be sealing my Fate with her. I already felt imprisoned in a life of servitude, never really enjoying the sense of freedom that comes with childhood.

We three kids were required to help the family, meaning we could not have the regular bonds we had with our friends like other children. Shawn represented that taste of freedom and a sense of normalcy. I was desperate to keep him in my life regardless of what my family thought of him. I needed a vehicle to transport me out of my lonely and oppressive home, and a boyfriend provided that.

MaryBelle took my arm and brought me to the living room as Bill and Shawn walked my mother to her car. We watched from the window as the two men stood at the curb, putting their hands on their hips like bookends to the other.

The sun had now set behind the trees, and an orange glow matched the fallen leaves being covered with fresh falling snow. We were supposed to be drinking hot chocolate and putting up Christmas decorations. The idyllic family portrait of the holidays, and now MaryBelle sat on the couch with her hand over her heart. I could tell the Teter family rarely had fits of anger or rage in their home. It was then I broke down and cried.

"I'm so sorry. I had no idea she would go this far!"

MaryBelle soothed me as a loving mother would, wrapping an arm around my shoulder and rubbing my back. "There, there," she cooed. "I can't fathom why your mother would do such a thing," she said, shaking her head. "Oh, Debbie, I had no idea how bad it was."

Bill and Shawn walked inside. Shawn motioned to me, and I went to him and received his protective embrace. We stood there for a long time in the living room, silent.

After my heartbeat returned to normal, I turned to Shawn's parents. "If you want me to leave, I will. I don't want this ever to happen again."

Bill spoke first, "Not in your life. You'll always have a place here with us, Debbie."

Tears rolled down my cheeks. MaryBelle rubbed my back, "You're like a daughter to us. I don't know what got into her mind about engagement. Bill and I agreed that you two should finish college before marriage. But it will be up to you two when you get engaged."

Bill added, "Besides, engagements can be broken at any time should you two decide that, too."

Shawn and I had talked about getting engaged before he left for his Spring semester in France. He was accepted during his junior year to attend James Madison's University in Paris. I transferred out of Mount Saint Mary's to attend community college at home until I could move to the University of Maryland in College Park the following Fall.

Mount Saint Mary's was a good school but lacked the courses I was interested in—my mother's last-ditch attempt to make me join a convent as a Nun.

Mount Saint Mary's was a Catholic college with a seminary on campus where young men attended to become Priests. She felt that if those of the Church could influence me, I, too, would turn to serve God for the remainder of my life. It would have been a sure ticket for her to get to Heaven, having a child of the Cloth. However, I was far from committing to God this way and felt He had other plans for me.

Shawn's early Christmas gifts to me pushed my mother over the edge. They symbolized too much. In her eyes, they were the closest thing to a proposal.

During the first weekend home from break, Shawn didn't want to wait for Christmas Day to surprise me. His parents were sitting by the freshly cut Christmas tree when he handed me the boxes.

First, I received a dainty gold wire ring with a tiny white pearl wrapped within the wire band. It was his 'promise ring' to me that we would get married after college. He then gave me a gold Mizpah Coin with the prayer of Genesis 31:49 engraved inside two hearts. The coins were split in half so each person could wear the other half. Inside the heart, it said, "Lord, watch between me and thee while we are absent one from another." We wore them every day after receiving them.

I spent the rest of the week shopping with his parents, only going home to sleep at night. It was the only way to see him since I couldn't have him in my home. My mother didn't think dating was necessary as a teenager.

Not having the opportunity to meet and interact with guys my age caused me to miss out on the invaluable practice of discerning what was good for me and what was not in my best interest. Sadly, I only learned the essential lessons of romantic relationships after meeting my first husband.

I had no prior knowledge of dating except what I saw in Saturday morning movies featuring Dean Martin, Cary Grant, Doris Day, and Audrey Hepburn. Unfortunately, my reality was that males behaved decades younger than the world portrayed in those movies, and the rules of etiquette were different.

I had met Shawn at a Freshman dance. He was friends with my neighbor, Lauren, who had met him at a party the summer before. She flirted with him as I stood there and watched their easy interaction until he left to seek out his group of friends.

I'm not sure if it was his cockiness that drew me in or if it was his hazel eyes that made my stomach do flip-flops, but I felt an instant connection with him. My heart raced when I saw him again in the hallways with his friends. He'd wink at me like we shared a secret, and it was all I needed to ensure we'd bump into each other again each day.

I'd map out his classes and make sure I was in his general vicinity in the lunchroom. He'd nod his head across the room or throw me a kiss. Even though I watched him do this with other girls, it felt like our connection was more profound, or so I had hoped.

Shawn had plenty of female friends; his art of flirtation was the highlight of their day. He was a charmer and knew how to work a room. I only knew about him through Lauren's tales of her summer philandering. Although she was a year younger than me, she had many experiences with boys and knew how they ticked. Shawn had shown interest in her, but she had her eyes on a senior football player.

Lauren introduced me to Shawn at the dance, and he and I became friends that year. I say friends since he would tell me about the girls he had crushes on. I knew, however, that these girls were out of his reach, their eyes on the upperclassmen. I would be patient until he finally noticed me as *the one*.

Shawn was tall, which made him intriguing, and his dark hair set off his hazel eyes. His confidence hewn from years of being known as the son of Mr. Teter, the best music teacher in the whole school district. Shawn owned the halls with much adoration. Yet, it was his slightly tucked chin and a somewhat less hard body than his friends that had missed the mark to complete the whole package of a studly Jock.

I applied for the manager position for the high school basketball and baseball teams, ensuring a daily interaction with him. Away tournaments meant we would sit close. A lingering touch or longing look in my direction sent chills down my spine and heat in my stomach. Those were fond memories of finding happiness between the long days of winter.

Things changed, however, when I went into the hospital unexpectedly due to a collapsed lung. The nurses allowed phone calls in the evening if I promised to rest after the day's last meal. Three long days of X-rays and tests showed the emergency room surgery didn't keep the lung up, so I needed surgery to repair the injured lung.

Shawn was my respite. He would call after his basketball practices, telling me how much he missed seeing me in the locker room and bleachers. He made me playlists and dropped them off at the nurses' station to pass on to me without my mother knowing. He colored the band's covers with my name woven inside the artwork. Our calls were filled with flirtations and innuendos, leaving me flushed and happy despite blood gushing from the drainage lines in my side.

I had turned 16 and knew it was time to learn about boys. I wasn't the boy-crazed type like my girlfriends, yet I knew something about his hazel eyes, black hair, and exceptional height that made me feel protected and loved.

I let him flirt with the other girls, though it never felt right if I admit it. I didn't know how to assert that side of myself —to be treated with respect and loyalty. So, when Shawn and I were in Study Hall, he'd meander through the room chatting it up with the other girls, their giggles disturbing our Social Studies teacher, Mr. Congdon, listening to the latest sports analysis on his small radio. I could feel a tiny ember of jealousy burn inside when Shawn would laugh a little too hard or move a lock of hair out of a girl's face.

Luckily, the other girls never went too far with their coy advances. I could see their glances toward me to see if anything on my face showed a semblance of jealousy. They liked me enough not to hurt me that way, and I think Shawn felt their allegiance, too, walking back to my table to attend to his girlfriend, who was all too happy to have him back.

These small, inane experiences taught me so little about dating and relationships. I held on to Shawn as more of a savior since being in love or dating in my home was forbidden. I would adore him so I could receive his graces for getting me out of my oppressive home.

So, when I did announce to my parents that Shawn and I were dating, they immediately told me they wouldn't condone his presence in their home.

I often wondered if I would have stayed together with him so long if it wasn't for my mother's constant pull to tear us apart. It was like the Montagues and Capulets, a continuous battle of Shawn and me desperately trying to see each other. We would sneak late-night phone calls to hear each other's voices until I heard the click on the other line. My mother incessantly eavesdropped on our conversations.

I would wait at night to hear the two beeps of his Honda Civic passing our home and then wait the thirteen minutes it took him to get home. Then, I would sneak downstairs to the phone in the kitchen. This way, I could hear if my mother got up from bed from the squeaky floorboards in their bedroom.

Our relationship grew even more once we were in college. We could dream of a future together, though something began to turn in my mind about what he wanted in a marriage. We were comfortable with each other, though I wasn't sure if I wanted the cozy family life he always spoke about. For now, though, I was happy to dream of having a loving family home.

Although Shawn was a good person, I needed someone with the same visions of traveling and exploring the world, which was a strong pull for me even at a young age. I also needed to learn that I deserved true love from someone who could hold me up and want the best for me. Nevertheless, I held on to him to prove I was worthy of someone's love regardless of the conditions it put me in.

I wished my parents had supported me and given me loving advice. They would have helped me realize that I deserved more than he could offer and see the flaws in our relationship.

However, the holier-than-thou looks I would get from my older sister, Sable, made me hold on to him even harder. I needed him to escape our oppressive home— how could she not recognize that? She would smirk at Shawn's less-than-polished graces when speaking to my parents when he walked me to the door. She disapproved of him, and she let my parents know each and every time. I saw what she saw, yet I rebelled against conforming to her wishes.

Shawn was brave enough to walk into the foyer and say hello. He spoke respectfully, though his chewing gum should have been tossed into the grass before stepping inside. He would kiss me on my cheek and leave. It was the most we could do to show them he was good to me.

When I showed my father Shawn's gifts that week, my dad said they were pretty, put his hands in his pockets, and walked away. I think he wanted to avoid the verbal assault my mother would impose on me once she saw them. It didn't take long.

I was in the kitchen taking a book out of my bookbag to read upstairs. I wanted to ease into the night with my happy thoughts of my perfect week with the Teter family and stay out of sight.

My mother walked into the kitchen and looked directly at my neck. My father must have mentioned it.

"Look what Shawn got for me!" I said, hoping my excitement would quell any scolding. "He also got me this little ring. Isn't it pretty?" I was smart enough to wear it on my right hand in front of her, though he had slipped it onto my left ring finger the night he gave it to me.

Her lips pressed into their deep crevasses, her black eyebrows knitting together. "You two are acting engaged!" she roared. Her face reddened.

"Mom, it's just a necklace and ring. Besides, it's a Catholic necklace. The Mizpah coin. He asked Father Timothy for ideas for a nice Christmas gift, and Father Tim showed him the coins."

I don't know why I mentioned that part. Trying to appease her Catholic side didn't seem to help. "He's going to be gone all next semester in France, so we will miss Valentine's Day," I said, trying to reason with her.

"I want you two to stop it. I don't like it!"

Shawn wasn't even Catholic. Though his father played the piano and sang for several churches in town, that was the closest the family ever came to religion. Shawn felt that maybe attending Mass with me would kill two birds with one stone. Spending time together innocently holding hands, Shawn would earn brownie points with the Priests, who would tell Mom they saw us together and always mention to her that he was very respectful.

She left the kitchen. I heard her storm upstairs. She was directly above me in their bedroom, where I could hear muffled yelling. It was only my mother yelling. My father only had short, low responses, and then the noise stopped. I heard her drag the desk chair out where she sat down, knowing she was displacing my father from watching his online stocks. Soon after, I heard his footsteps come down the stairs. He stopped at the kitchen door, getting my attention by waving his hand at me.

I shrugged my shoulders, asking him silently what I did wrong.

He also shrugged his shoulders and threw his hands down in defeat as if throwing down any semblance of trying to understand his wife's rants against his daughter.

I hated seeing him so downtrodden. He was always a jolly man, yet my mother brought everyone down with her control and tirades. I also wished he would stand up for me. It wasn't like I was taking drugs or causing mayhem. I wanted to date a boy I liked and who liked me back.

I could tell he just wanted to settle in and watch the news, so I grabbed my book, snuck upstairs, and closed my bedroom door.

I knew, however, it wasn't over. My mother would sit and simmer for days until the third day, and she would get angry again. It was her pattern. I always thought of Jesus during the days leading up to her new wrath and wondered if her three-day wait had anything to do with the Bible. However, instead of her coming to an understanding or developing compassion over those several days, it was another rage against what she could not control.

Both my twin brother and sister understood it, too. It was crucial to be away from our Mom three days after any event that led to her gavel of judgment coming crashing down. This time, however, she got bold.

Shawn's parents invited me to the house three days after giving me my gifts to make Christmas cookies and cinnamon quick bread as traditional Christmas movies played on the television. It was an idyllic Currier and Ives scene at the Teter home, complete with carols.

Then my mother stormed in to let the world know her daughter was an abnormality in her eyes, shamefully dating in college, and that I should be banished to a convent.

After my mother left, MaryBelle and I sat and talked. She asked me about my mother's dating years. What I knew was vague. My mother didn't reveal much about that time, but I knew she had a few suitors. Her jewelry drawer was filled with beautiful necklaces, bracelets, and pins, which were given to her by several men she had attended dances. However, there was one ring I felt told a more romantic and tragic story.

It was a two-carat solitaire diamond ring with offset baguette diamonds on each side of the solitaire. She used to tell us it was a cocktail ring. However, knowing my mother had worked in a furniture store and other benign jobs, women in the 1950s would only own a diamond ring of that size if it was an engagement ring. The offset baguettes were also set in a way that allowed a wedding band to surround them.

"I think she was engaged, and the man broke her heart," I told MaryBelle of my conclusion. "She met my father when she was in her late twenties."

MaryBelle turned to Bill, who was listening on the couch, his feet on the coffee table. "That is quite old for back then," he agreed.

"They were married three months after he returned from his expedition in Antarctica. The Navy promoted him, and he was supposed to go again for another six-month tour, but she demanded he quit the Navy and come home to get married."

MaryBelle shifted in her seat. "You would think she would want her daughters to have experience dating men. To be able to learn how to choose wisely. That's what dating is all about. It still makes me reel, what she did to you during Prom. To purposefully leave the film out of the camera while taking pictures of you and Shawn is beyond my comprehension. I think there is some real concern when it comes to her mental health."

"Well, at least you and Bill took some photos, so we have those," I said meekly.

Bill cleared his throat, "Well, there is something not right if a parent does something so dishonest for control."

He stood from his seat, "Who wants a bowl of ice cream with pretzels on top?"

I didn't rush home that night.

Shawn and I sat on the loveseat facing the television and Christmas tree. Bill read the newspaper, and MaryBelle sat on the couch doing some crossword puzzles when she excitedly put her book down.

MaryBelle smiled, "Now, I think this is as good a time as ever to show you something I've been working on." She hurried up the stairs and, a moment later, walked down with a large, framed piece of artwork in her hands. Shawn beamed knowingly, helping her turn the sizable antique gold frame around to face me.

Inside the frame was a gorgeous cross-stitch portrait of a Victorian gazebo in a floral garden setting, with giant purple hyacinths framing it. Shawn's name was stitched inside the gazebo in large letters, and an intricate ampersand was stitched in the middle. I could see ever so faintly the letters of my name penciled under his.

She grinned at the men in the room as Bill and Shawn held up the frame. I was speechless. MaryBelle has cross-stitched the most beautiful wedding announcement for all to see.

"Shawn knows I've been working on this for almost a year. That's why I asked you about your favorite colors and flowers a long time ago."

Shawn took my hand as I admired his mother's handiwork.

"You knew about this?" I said, my voice faint.

He winked at me, wiping a tear from his mother's cheek. "Yup. She knew how much you loved gazebos, and it fits the length of your name, too."

I hugged her. At that moment, I knew that no matter what happened to Shawn and me in the years to come, his parents would always have a special place in my heart.

Bill took my necklace and fixed the broken link. He and Shawn then went to the garage to retrieve some outdoor Christmas decorations we had planned to put out that night.

They lit winter-scented candles as Bill sang Christmas songs. His soprano voice carried throughout the house. It was times like these, doing family traditions, when I felt closest to the Teter family. This family gave me a taste of normalcy and familial love that I could not experience at home. I was allowed to witness balance, love, and compassion, all absent in my life.

Shawn drove me home that night. He pulled into the driveway, and we sat for as long as possible before my father opened the garage door. It was almost like my father was giving me the all-clear to sneak inside and go to bed without my mother knowing.

"I'll come get you tomorrow," Shawn said, "and we can go to Peddler's Village with my folks. The gingerbread houses are on display, and my mom thought it would be fun for us to go see them."

I smiled, so thankful for him and his family. It was Christmas break, and we promised to see each other as much as possible before he returned to James Madison University.

I knew, though, that no matter what, I had to stay away from my mother at all costs. Shawn picked me up every day during our break, and I would spend the day with him and his family, enjoying our little town of Doylestown in its Christmas glory. It was completely decorated for Christmas in a way that can only be described as a quintessential New England Christmas town. Each storefront lit candles in its windows, and ornate pine and berry boughs draped over hearths and doorways.

Christmas carolers strolled the snowy cobblestoned pathways, and chestnut vendors roasted their fragrant nuts over their fires. Perfect families gathered around perfect fires, eating s'mores and hot candied cinnamon almonds.

I only went home to go to sleep, avoiding my parents as much as I could. Once Shawn left for France, I knew I would be cloistered until Spring break. I realized I would only be free once I graduated from college, so until then, I made plans to free myself from them.

***

This was a pivotal moment for me at nineteen, days away from turning twenty. The grassy sod of my childhood was peeled away, and the dirt, rocks, and knotty roots were laid bare for all to see. I could have left the sod alone and given the illusion of the well-manicured lawn of my family.

My mother would say, "Smile and keep them guessing," keeping the illusion of a happy family intact when, in reality, we were all playing out a facade to the outside world. I refused to live in a lie and allow them to contort the fact that we were a dysfunctional family.

Wallowing in this muck could have been another choice. I could have feigned being a victim until I believed it. I could rewire my brain to blame my mother for all the disasters in my life and continue as a broken adult destined to play out victimhood in every self-created crisis.

I could create allies that repeated my miserable story repeatedly so that I could relive it and then blame my parents for any shortcomings. Those allies would perpetuate the story since it's a fact of humanity that people love to look at how infested another person's garden is compared to their own. It's easier to allow a person to believe their lies than to break the pattern of deceit, enabling them to continue with their skewed perceptions.

These allies I speak of are like the rocks in the soil, deterring the growth of healthy seeds. The friends we surround ourselves with have a purpose other than companionship. They are our mirror. They show us who we really are, and if they are not strong enough to counter any lie you tell yourself, then you are creating a garden of false perceptions and beliefs.

I would rather have friends who tell me when I'm thinking incorrectly than those who perpetuate a story that stunts my growth.

I realized my mother was on her own journey of discovery. It was up to her to dig away at the decades of weeds overgrown into a field of denial. Uncovering these truths meant she would have to look at herself and all she contributed, causing her garden to turn to weeds with the overgrowth of judgment and distorted beliefs.

She was a product of her upbringing, though I did not witness that time in her life. It wasn't fair of me to label her as crazy but to point out that she was a human on the same journey of self-discovery.

She was a woman dealing with her own demons from childhood, whether real or imagined. I would learn in her later years that her fears were born at a very young age, during the Second World War and a time when children were expected to listen to their parents and follow the traditions of their religion.

She hung onto her fears like a blanket of snow covering a dormant patch of earth, protecting her from whatever she thought would get her now, an adult woman, thousands of miles away from those shadows under her windowpanes. Her fears were part of her story, and she was willing to participate in her play.

Her garden never flourished. She never had a Spring where she confronted those irrational childhood fears.

My father wasn't willing to help her confront them either and let her live with them instead. He indulged her beliefs, avoiding as much conflict as possible. He was her ally and helped perpetuate a skewed view of the world. Although he did it out of love and fear of conflict, his lack of standing up for me and my brother from my mother and older sister created a family full of anger, sadness, and dysfunction. Sadly, her fears and beliefs were all she had left when my father passed years later.

Once I was on my own, I knew it was essential to create distinctions between my family and others, recognizing the different forms of parenting, friendships, and alliances. This helped me understand that for some people in my life, I would need to let them go, send them love, and allow them to plant their own garden without me.

Composting:

Compost is a process of mixing ingredients to create a plant fertilizer that improves the soil's physical, chemical, and biological properties. It is commonly prepared by decomposing plant and food waste and recycling organic materials and manure. The resulting mixture is rich in plant nutrients and beneficial organisms, such as bacteria, protozoa, nematodes, and fungi. Compost improves soil fertility in gardens, landscaping, horticulture, urban agriculture, and organic farming, reducing dependency on man-made engineered chemical fertilizers.

CHAPTER TWO

What grows in a compost pile?

HOW DEATH BRINGS NEW LIFE

There comes a time when you reflect on your purpose and why you exist. This hit me when I turned 30 and the years following. I realized I only had a set period of time on this grand Earth and wanted it to count. This type of reflection depends on the belief systems put in place as a young person. For many, this reflection of where you fit in the world may never happen for fear of the answers it may reveal.

If you believe everything is based on chance, you also think you can't create change. This is like being given a gorgeous plot of barren land, yet nothing is done to cultivate it and allow it to flourish. Is it by chance that it doesn't receive any water, or the seeds don't germinate?

Whenever you feel unsure about your ability to bring about long-lasting change, I highly recommend watching the inspiring documentary *"The Biggest Little Farm."* This documentary follows John and Molly Chester and their dog Todd, who decide to leave their city life behind and create a sustainable farm in harmony with Nature. Through their struggles and successes, they demonstrate how small changes can significantly impact the environment and the community. It's a heartwarming and informative film that will empower you to make positive changes in your life.

The lofty aspirations of creating a diverse farm in perfect harmony with Nature face numerous challenges, including depleted soil, loss of animals, devastating drought, and a wildfire that threatens the farm. For eight years, the couple worked tirelessly to achieve their vision, planting thousands of orchard trees and hundreds of different crops and bringing in various animals - one of which is an unforgettable pig named Emma and her feisty companion, Greasy the rooster. As the farm begins to thrive again, so does the Chesters' hope for a utopian existence. However, unexpected events force them to reevaluate their ideological approach to truly understand the complexities and wisdom of Nature and life itself to survive.

None of this was easy; Mother Nature is an intricate force, constantly creating and changing, sometimes without a beneficial conclusion — or so we think. One thing is guaranteed, however: the Chesters have learned, failed, and gained much wisdom on their journey. That is what they came here to do. They had a nugget of a dream and allowed their thoughts, dreams, and desires to bring it to fruition.

Understanding and acknowledging the importance of being aware of your thoughts, actions, and surroundings is crucial to creating a fertile ground for growth and improvement in all aspects of your life. This concept, referred to as 'tilth,' emphasizes the quality of the soil that nurtures the seeds of growth and success in the same way that your awareness and mindfulness play a vital role in cultivating your desired lifestyle, relationships, and achievements.

Being intentional and conscious of your choices, decisions, and behaviors can create a solid foundation for your personal and professional development. However, it takes toil and hardship to recognize *you* must be the farmer. It's up to you to make the change.

You are the change – not the barren land. The land is just ready to receive your efforts.

Composting serves as a powerful symbol of personal growth and transformation. By embracing and engaging with life's challenges, you can turn your experiences into valuable lessons that nourish your personal development. Just as composting creates nutrient-rich soil for beautiful gardens to flourish, you can cultivate resilience, wisdom, and strength to produce beautiful gardens in your life.

However, there is something to say about the material compost is made of. Compost is created by dead and decomposing plant material. This is gathered over time from garden debris or brought in as manure from horses, cows, chickens, pigs, and other animals' waste. It sits, ferments, and breaks down everything it once was to become a rich and nurturing soil. Mother Nature knows it takes death to renew life. However, the pile could sit and never be used. It would then just become one big pile of shit. What you choose to do with all that material can grow your path.

I could have chosen to stay in a place where I blamed all of my faults, trials, and hardships on my mother or sister. However, they were there to play a role in my life. Even during those times, I questioned the purpose of these onslaughts I endured. I knew there had to be a reason I was born into a family with these issues.

This lifetime is our school, and we came to learn lessons to advance our Soul's learning. Being on a planet as a physical being creates natural consequences for every action taken. Like gravity, there is a push and pull to every choice we make, and the greatest lessons I had to learn were to create boundaries with the members of my family and people I would meet along the way.

I also learned about the human need to protect certain belief systems, even if those beliefs harm a person's wellbeing and growth. This understanding helped me realize that everyone is here to learn, and sometimes, we must let people do just that—learn—without our input or participation.

I believe that we are here to explore the intricacies of human relationships. Moreover, I am of the opinion that we have chosen our families even before we were born. If we did not make this choice, then the lessons we learn in life would be purely random. We can test this theory by observing the patterns of recurring life lessons we face until we finally understand them.

Reflecting on my beginnings and hardships, each trauma I experienced had a thread of sameness. I needed to learn to feel worthy enough to set boundaries on how people treated me. I also needed to understand that although a person has a role, like Mother, Father, Sister, or even Twin Brother, I had to learn that the expectations put upon those roles were false and no longer served me or them.

So, like everything we experience in life, there will be a death of some sort. The end of a marriage, a healthy body, or the death of a loved one. It could also be the death of a belief, like our expectations of our parents or friends or a religion.

These deaths, however, aren't there to only reveal loss. They are there to teach us the impermanence of our existence and give us lessons. Ironically, these lessons were taught to me by my mother, sister, and other people who would enter my life.

Letting go of a family member to no longer have jurisdiction over your life is freeing. It gave me the fortitude to stand up for myself and what I needed most: autonomy. As soon as I realized this, the path I was meant to be on would reveal itself to me, and it was awe-inspiring.

I was thirty years old and a new mother. McKenzie was born through a difficult birth, and I felt so blessed this little girl chose me to be her mom. However, my marriage of ten years had proven to be challenging, with bouts of abuse and emotional turmoil. I had met McKenzie's father in college and was enamored with his potential. He could command a room with his energetic charisma, but I learned he was a man with a dark shadow cast upon his heart behind closed doors.

I hadn't planned on having children with him. I wanted to explore the world and live experiences that rivaled my brother and sister's adventures. It was also less than ideal since he had already failed at two marriages, one with a son he never got to see.

Then, suddenly, without any provocation, I desired to have a child. I remember it being out of the blue, and an unexpectedly joyous feeling washed over me. However, I was with a man who was less than an ideal husband. I pushed the thought away, although my heart hurt thinking I'd never be blessed with motherhood. Life set things in motion when an unexpected vacation gave us McKenzie.

The first few months were glorious, doting over our little brown-eyed, brown-haired girl. I felt so connected to this little being in my care, like a lioness and her cub, watchful and protective. Jack, however, became distant, and I realized our days together were numbered. His physical aggression toward me became worse. I had endured unexpected bouts of his abuse before McKenzie was born, but it now became more frequent. I didn't want my little cub to be in the line of his hostility, so I met with a lawyer and secretly planned my divorce.

I decided to have my mother watch McKenzie while Jack and I took a weekend trip so I could tell him of my plans to divorce him. Things, however, went differently than planned — another lesson in setting boundaries. Jack and I were forced to get home due to my mother's meddling in our affairs. I had just started telling him about us possibly going our separate ways when his parents called our hotel room. They told us to rush home due to my mother 'going insane.'

I pulled up to the departure lane at the airport, watching my mother's reaction. Her hands laid over her black purse on her lap in indignation. She had a cowlick of black hair standing in the back of her head from her short wedge haircut. Although she'd comb it down, it always had a mind of its own and stood at an angle to the rest of her hair. In a sense, that cowlick defined my mother. She was contradictory to the norms of who a mother should be by her judgemental beliefs and desperate need for control.

Her face told me all I needed to know. She was completely ignoring the reality of what she did to me.

She was silent for the majority of the drive. It only took me twenty minutes to get to the airport, so I knew my words had to be poignant. I turned in my seat to face her. She kept her gaze forward.

"Mom, I told you that I had everything taken care of. I had met with the lawyer, and I had the documents of the abuse all in order. My trip with Jack was to tell him that I was divorcing him for good. I needed to get him away from McKenzie into neutral territory. That's why I asked you to fly out here and watch her for me."

"But Debbie, the things he did to you."

"Mom, I had it all under control. I was planning on handing him those divorce papers you found under my bed when we returned from the trip. If you only kept things quiet."

"But that's my granddaughter, and I have grandparent rights."

"Mom, you don't have any rights to take over something you had no right to take over! Now Jack knows my plan of divorcing him and can prepare. You took that from me. Now I have to be on guard. I can't just leave now, since you tipped off his parents. How far did you get with your phone calls anyway?"

She looked out the window, shaking her head. "Oh, not that many," she said snidely. "Just a few people. Your cousin, who's a lawyer, and Jack's parents."

I watched a plane land in the distance. My cheeks flushed, knowing my cousins, whom I only saw on rare occasions, must think of me as the poor helpless cousin my sister tried to convince them of so many years ago. And Jack's parents must have been shocked by the news of their son's impending third divorce.

I continued, "Yes, they called Jack immediately once you called them. You took away my ability to keep me and McKenzie safe. Now Jack knows and that was the one thing the lawyer said was on my side."

"Well, I'm sorry, Debbie," she said through clenched teeth. I could tell it was hard for her to apologize like it was something so bitter, like bile forming in her mouth. "I didn't know. So you can't blame me for not knowing."

She was bent on defending her side. However, I realized she was stuck in a perception she could not break. She was a prisoner to what her mind told her to think. She was so stuck in her beliefs that she couldn't see the big picture of what her actions could do to someone. I realized then she was so attached to her own reality that it didn't match the rest of the world.

"Mom, it would be one thing if it was all innocent like you believe. But I am making you leave because you have overstepped your bounds with me, and I can't trust you have my best interest at hand. You called my co-workers, my boss, my friends, and even my cousins who have no idea what I've been through! I can't fathom what made you want to do this knowing it could damage me! I have already been through enough, and now you are throwing more gasoline into the mix."

I stopped. My voice was getting tight, and I didn't want to yell. No more yelling for her to hear me as I did as a little girl. This was my life now, and she had no more control over me. I had moved three thousand miles away from her. This was my sanctuary now.

I started again calmly, "Well, now you know you've put me in a worse situation than I was before. It may take months to leave him safely without involving more people."

I could tell I hit a nerve. It had always been like this, this breaking of wills. She had nothing more to say to defend herself. Her voice got small, like her brain began to decipher, allowing her to comprehend some small part of her actions. But it wasn't about her understanding the other person's plight. It was about how it affected her.

"Well, I guess I won't be seeing my granddaughter again, will I?"

"Mom, it will take some time before I can have you here. I need to get things in order, and I'm not sure how long that will take. I'm not taking McKenzie away from you, but I need time to undo all that you did."

Meekly, she added, "Well, again, I'm sorry," her eyes filled with tears this time.

It was the first time I remember my words getting to her like this. I felt the shedding of the last thirty-one years fall off of me like the skin of a snake, slowly unwinding all the pain and anguish she caused me over the years. Maybe this was my time to take control of my life and only allow her in it if it was on my terms now.

I pulled the car up to SkyCab and opened the door for her. I took out her suitcase and stood in front of her. It was the first time in my adult life I had stood up to this woman in a manner that made me see her in a completely different light. She was a smaller, more meek form of herself, and her capacity to control my life was gone. I had finally challenged her, and it felt empowering.

I had tried many times to free myself from her grasp. And although there were times I got close, it always came down to me being a minor and living in their home. This time, it was my house and my rules, and I put her on the next flight home to my dad in Pennsylvania.

It was awkward showing up to work that morning. My colleagues looked at me with caution. I didn't know exactly how many people she called from my address book, but the glances in the hallway made it easy to guess. My principal, Steven Hall, called me into his office and had me sit down.

He had known me for over seven years, and I considered him a friend. His face showed concern as he sat down behind his desk.

"So, I wasn't expecting to hear from your mother this weekend," he said, holding his hands in prayer, his fingertips grazing his mustache. "Weren't you on a trip to Napa?"

I looked out the window to see students rushing to the playground and my friend Janice walking in with other teachers.

"I guess I was lucky she stopped at the H's in my address book." I shake my head and chuckle.

He pushed his chair back, propping his arms onto the arms of the chair.

"And, yes, I was planning on giving Jack the divorce papers this weekend, but didn't want McKenzie nearby. I figured having my mom there watching McKenzie would keep things from going too far South with him, if you know what I mean."

The school counselor, Katie Lands, rushed into Steven's office, shut the door, and immediately sat beside me. I had known her for the same seven years I had been teaching and always felt she was an ally. She and Steven also knew Jack, so it was a shock that there were problems.

Jack was a master of disguise. He could make everyone believe we were a perfect couple. Still, once alone in our home, he shed the mask of tranquility and became an emotionally distant, controlling, abusive partner.

"Debbie, I'm so sorry this happened. But your mom seemed a little off. I mean, almost psychotic!" she laughed uneasily, then looked at Steven.

"She called you, too?" he asked. "Must have your maiden name in the phone book."

Katie looked confused.

He shook his head, "Hopkins, instead of Lands. She called everyone up to the H's in Debbie's address book."

"Oh! You've got to be kidding," Katie paused, putting her hand over her mouth.

"Don't feel bad about laughing, Katie. That's all I've got at the moment," I said.

"Yes! Laughing is good. She was going on about things I had no idea you were going through! Jack's abuse and emotional harm! Debbie, I can get you the help you need to get out of the house!"

I smiled, trying to put them at ease. I had been dealing with this irrational woman for thirty-one years. It was nothing new. As for Jack, I had a plan. A carefully executed plan to leave him for good. But now that was dangling precariously.

"Yeah, kinda crazy, huh? But you get used to it," I said, trying to make light of the situation.

Katie reached over and touched my arm, "But, if what she says is true, are you and your daughter safe from him? Is he still hurting you?"

I paused at that moment, knowing it showed on my face. It felt too close, that question. I had been holding my own for the past seven years, yet now, with my seven-month-old daughter, I knew I needed to break away from him finally. He had always broken things around me so that I could brush that off. But when I began standing up for myself, he came after me. I knew then I had to leave with our daughter before he turned against her, too.

"I am making plans on getting McKenzie and me out of the situation. But it will take some time to get things back in order. And, now, with Mom interfering with my escape, so to speak, I have to rework some things."

Katie stood up and motioned me to the door. "Let's go back to your classroom and maybe set up a plan for you and McKenzie to be safe."

Steven nods in agreement, "I want you to know you have a lot of resources here, if you need them."

He was a stern principal to many teachers he didn't care for, and I was thankful he respected me and our friendship to reach out.

"Thanks for that," I stood by the door before opening it. "Well, my mother's on a plane home now, so I'm hoping things will calm down."

Katie turned to Steven, "I've never experienced such a crazy phone call. I can't imagine what people were thinking when they got the call?"

My face flushed at the thought of my dirty laundry being revealed to all. It must have shown.

Steven slowly nodded, "Katie will make sure any fires your mom may have started will be put out immediately."

Katie grabbed my hand, "Absolutely! You have enough on your plate as is, dealing with an abusive husband. You don't need stress here at work. I'll be sure to squash any talk."

Walking into my classroom was a strange sensation. There wasn't a place my mother's fire hadn't touched. I was 2,000 miles away in Colorado, and yet her impact was palatable in my space.

I felt like a crack had been exposed in my facade. People now knew I didn't have it all together, which strangely seemed liberating. For years, I had tried to hide the emotional and physical abuse I faced from my husband. Now, it also revealed how dysfunctional my family was.

As a young girl, I always understood that something wasn't right with my mother. I discovered too young that the hero complex most children have of their parents was squashed for me. Witnessing the family dynamics of my neighbors, friends, and my high school sweetheart's family showed me how twisted my family was. I needed to get out. My issues with Jack seemed almost secondary. I had a plan, albeit exposed. It was a plan that made me feel empowered.

Katie closed my classroom door behind me. We only had a few minutes to talk before the playground bell rang.

She spoke kindly, and I saw what made her a good counselor. She revealed she went through the same thing with her ex-husband and what she did to protect her and her daughter.

I walked over to my filing cabinet and unlocked it. I showed Katie a folder that contained my lawyer's documents about the assaults. I also showed her a metal lockbox where I put cash for the 'just in case.' I shared how I opened a separate bank account so I could get an apartment quickly. However, I originally planned to stay with my sister Sable in California.

Katie reminded me that staying with my sister might not be the best move since he knew where she lived and would likely try to find us. I was also leaving the state without a court order. Luckily, I had changed my mind about staying with Sable. Although my sister and I had tried to reconcile over the years, I knew I might lose the boundaries I had built to protect myself from controlling people. She and my mother were two seeds from the same pod.

As Katie left my classroom, I felt a sense of relief that my struggles were no longer hidden and that I could now seek help. Looking back, I tried to reach out to mutual friends but was often met with awkward resistance. Our friends hesitated to take sides and had to weigh the consequences of supporting my ex-husband, who was also their friend, or me.

If anything, my mother's actions solidified that I knew the days were numbered in my marriage, and with careful planning, I could move on without too much damage to myself or my daughter.

Jack did stop coming after me physically. After my mom left, his behavior was typically remorseful, like giving me flowers or taking me out to dinner to 'try to reconnect.'

It was easy to let days and weeks go by without any confrontations since he was busy teaching and coaching. Our days melded into a blur of obligations, and my evenings, when he was gone to the Sports Books, gave me time to start my new hobby of writing. It was cathartic and freeing to find comfort in words, in my thoughts, with all that pressed upon my mind and heart.

It also allowed me to plan better financially. I applied for my Master's and National Board Certification in teaching since it would provide me the financial boost I would need as a soon-to-be single mother. I decided to better prepare myself for the inevitable and allow Jack's gambling to be an excuse for why we never saw each other.

Katie and Steven kept tabs on me. They figured Jack and I reconciled, and in a sense, we did. Jack was gone most of the time coaching, so it was easy for my daughter and me to fall into another life of doing things by ourselves. It was the beginning of being a single, married woman. I lived life with my daughter between the obligatory meals and events that married couples do and quietly made my plans to leave him for good—finally.

I also needed time to shed the veil of my Catholic Faith. I realized that it was holding me back from leaving Jack. Did I give my marriage the effort it required? He wasn't hurting me anymore. Instead, things like a crystal vase or glass frame on the credenza laid victim to his anger.

"Catholics don't divorce," my sister-in-law, Tatiana, once told me. But she didn't know the extent of my suffering to understand that such archaic dogmas no longer served me. My brother's wife was another person I had to contend with.

Tatiana was very devout to the Church. Her parents were deeply intertwined in the Faith, so my brother's wife frowned upon my considering divorce. She elaborated extensively on the factors I needed to consider regarding McKenzie's potential future as a child of divorced parents. I don't ever recall her asking how bad it was with Jack and trying to understand what I had gone through, but that would mean she would have to have empathy and compassion toward me, and that was something she was not going to give her husband's twin.

Leaving Jack wasn't something I took lightly since I had taught many children from divorced families. I knew the ramifications if I didn't consider her wellbeing. But it was like Tati to assume I was careless—she heard my sister's opinions of me, so why should Tati think differently? I did have to undo the wrong choice of picking my husband. However, even knowing I chose Jack, I knew there was a reason and lesson I had to comprehend to grow in this life. Maybe it was to have McKenzie — and her growth as a Soul also had to be considered.

I had a few run-ins with Tatiana's temper, so it was best to let it lie. I let Tati know that I had the permission of three priests to leave my abusive marriage — all being willing to help me with the annulment should I need it. She was surprised but rambled on about drug addiction, promiscuity, and such.

My parents believed that being Catholic was a priority and that attending weekly Mass, Catechism classes, and Confession was necessary for a good Catholic. It was not just a Christian thing to do, but Catholic, like it held a little more weight in Heaven.

It was all just a mystery to me. Men and women in black and white vestments have exclusive rights to God's ear, like Santa Claus and his elves.

Most of it was a tedious series of rituals and traditions. It was comfortable and cozy, like a well-worn sweater, familiar with no frills, the same stories year after year, and sermons that would drone of ancient peoples and miracles that we don't seem to see today.

There was also a feeling of guilt if you didn't do things correctly: recite specific prayers, no meat Fridays, Novenas, and the like. Confession was downright horrifying at age seven after receiving First Communion. Sitting in a closet-sized room, fearful of the penance I had to perform from confessions I mostly made up. Although hitting Timothy Gothchild in the nose was well deserved, what great mortal sins could a small girl do?

Later, it occurred to me that lying about sins I didn't commit was most likely a sin, too. I would shrug my shoulders and realize I'd have to argue with Saint Peter at the Gate if this was a significant concern.

This is where I had the first whispers of doubt that such an incredible Being would demand such things to make us fear Him, if He was a He at all.

I wasn't uncomfortable with the name God. I felt He was too great, too large to have such a small, three-letter name. Three letters for something that created everything didn't seem glorious enough in my naïve mind.

To me, God was more of an all-encompassing energy surrounding every minute detail in the Universe. This energy, this Spirit, was inside everything, although humans tried to bottle it up and sell it to the people as their own.

My memories of Sundays were of starving before Mass since God must have you on an empty stomach to absorb His Word. It also didn't make sense that God could only be found on Sundays in a grand white building.

My thoughts would wander during the Homily to the Lions on the Serengeti in the Mutual of Omaha television specials we watched every Sunday night. Depending on which animal they were showcasing, we never witnessed animals gathering together once a week for prayer or contemplation on their latest kill. Where did it occur in Nature, the Nature God created, that penance should be served?

I couldn't comprehend why it was left to only humans to have such rituals, never seeing it demonstrated elsewhere in the Animal or Plant Kingdom. However, I also didn't have the confidence to challenge it, and if I did, would their God cast me off as a lost cause?

So, not wanting to test this enigmatic God, I would ride my bike up the winding hill to the Shrine of Our Lady of Czestochowa. I'd light candles and recite prayers until my mind went elsewhere. It was a source of comfort during my uncertain teen years when I needed security and guidance, but I had come to terms with it in my own way.

I would speak to the Saints, Jesus and Mary, like they were my dead relatives watching over me and ask if they could intervene on my behalf during those difficult times with my mother and sister. Although I felt they were listening, I thought I wasn't worthy enough to receive any blessings since I hadn't witnessed any great revelations or relief. This could be why I stayed with my husband, Jack, for years longer than I should have.

Believing that McKenzie and I deserved to be free of anguish and loneliness became my new devotion and prayer. I met with several Priests and presented my case that I must divorce to be safe and free. Each one gave me their blessings, and I was ready to take the next step.

I knew then this Church – although steeped in comforting traditions— was not my way forward.

Years passed, McKenzie got older, and she became wise to her father's inability to be an emotionally connected father to her and a husband to me. On a warm summer drive, McKenzie told me it was okay for me to divorce her father. She had witnessed the shell of a man who could not connect with his daughter and now gave me permission to be free.

Six months later, she and I were out on our own to breathe freely for the first time in my twenty years of marriage. She was now twelve and my rock in our new life together. I told her that my marriage to her father was my 'starter marriage,' a marriage to help you learn who you are and what you need in a relationship to flourish, and a starter marriage was meant to let go of when you learned all you were supposed to learn.

It's like rototilling a spent garden since it cannot provide the proper nourishment for growth for plants to survive. The divorce would allow a new garden to be prepared once the soil had a chance to breathe again.

I had learned to stand up for myself and realize I was worthy of being loved and to love myself. I loved the life I created for McKenzie and me and realized I had so much to offer the world as a teacher and a woman ready to start over and begin a new life.

I learned to care for myself by swimming in the evenings after work and taking time for quiet reflection and meditation. McKenzie also grew in developing interests for her self-growth, diving into yoga, orchestra, and theater.

I dove into cooking and learning about new places to explore with my daughter.

We were learning to till this new patch of soil and tend to the dirt with love, compassion, and forgiveness toward ourselves. We fed it our renewed excitement of the possibilities and planted seeds of dreams and journeys we wanted to explore. The soil was ready, and the seeds were ripening under this new season of our life.

Here is a link to watch The Biggest Little Farm, a movie that will delight everyone and maybe inspire you to grow something big! This link is a part of my Amazon Storefront. Enjoy!

Companion gardening:

The practice of growing different plants together for mutual benefit. While companion planting is a great way to get more yields out of your garden, you also need to pay attention to the opposite – which plants don't go well together.

Chapter Three

Companion Planting

Bittersweet unconditional love and loss

If I had to decide why my brother was in my life, it would be the reason to understand what unconditional love, protection, and loyalty were all about. I had to experience having someone in my life who always had my back, believed in me, and loved me no matter what. However, it is through the contrast of losing him in my life that I gained understanding and discernment.

Our relationship began at birth and exists today, although extremely different. I never thought that I would lose my brother, and not in the eternal sense.

Sometimes, like in gardening, you take for granted that your plants will grow. You nurtured them for years, giving them the same tender care and attention, and then one day, they turn yellow and die.

You've done nothing different in your gardening technique. Nothing changed in the soil. But then, suddenly, the plants no longer thrive. You realize too late that an outside influence altered the course of your garden's health, and you hopelessly watch it whither away and die.

This was the case with my twin. I realized forty years later that our separation was more a lesson for him to learn than for me. We often forget it's not always about us. Dane was on his path in life, and I was just a reflection of what he needed to learn. Although I know deep in my heart that he loves me as he always had, he would have to pursue why he chose to let go of his twin and whether it was a worthy cause or not. I could point out the obvious to him, but that is like forcing a tree to grow in one direction- it can be done but with much cutting and pruning and the risk of losing the tree altogether.

So, I wished him well and sent him loving thoughts.

The first memory I can recall in my life was of my twin brother, Dane. We were crawling down a small grassy hill on the side of our yard one summer afternoon. His white diaper and red curly hair shone brightly in the warm sun. I remember giggling and laughing, although I couldn't keep up with him. Something was wrong that kept me from being as fast as he was, yet he never left my side. He would stop and sit back as I slowly scooted forward.

Later, I learned I could not fully extend my hips due to the constriction of being in vitro with a twin. Luckily, I don't remember the pain of wearing leg braces for hours to correct the issue, and I never fell behind after that.

I remember us crawling toward newly planted white pine trees that lined the edge of our yard, then stopping and giggling more. The first memory of my constant companion was a feeling of happiness, protection, and being completely loved. My first memory fades at this point, and our mother picks me up.

Twins, indeed, have a special bond that can't be explained. To my older sister's chagrin, we spoke in a silly, made-up language. We laughed without speaking; we knew each other's thoughts. Years later, I would find myself humming a tune from The Wizard of Oz when his daughters were in the car with me. They all gaped and said their dad always hummed that same tune. They wondered if we hummed it simultaneously, although several thousand miles apart. I felt we did.

Our connection was apparent when he was physically hurt. As soon as I got the news, I would feel a rush of pain run up my legs as if my body were experiencing the same pain.

We were best friends growing up, always involved in what the other was doing. We would sneak into each other's cribs during our nap time by throwing a blanket over from his crib to mine. I would grab onto it, and he would pull our rolling cribs together. To our mother's surprise, she would find us laughing and playing together late into the night.

We would play for hours outside, in the basement, or exploring the nearby lake and forests. We would build forts from blankets or snow and create amazing adventures. If he took his shirt off, I would take off mine. We were six then, so it didn't make a difference. If he climbed a tree, I would follow without a second thought. Not a day would go by that we weren't on some adventure together.

He was my protector. There wasn't anything I could do where he wouldn't have my back. I remember fishing in the lake down the road, where we rode our bikes often. It was a hot, sticky summer day, and he knew where we could catch some bluegill. We parked our bikes at the top of a dam where the water rushed into a stream down onto the other side. There was a perfect rock-edged pond that spilled over before entering into the stream below. It was stocked with bluegill each year.

We set our hooks, dropped our lines, and watched the bobbers for the tell-tale sign of a bite. It was stiflingly hot, so we dipped our legs into the water, waiting for a fish to take the worm. Dane moved down the pond a little from me so our lines wouldn't cross. I slid into the water until I was up to my waist, trying to cool off, watching the ripples I created reach the far end of the pond. Suddenly, I saw something motion off the rocks and into the water. To my utter fear, two black water moccasins were swimming toward me.

I could barely make a sound. I desperately called for my brother, but I was paralyzed by fear. The only sound that came out of my mouth was, "Duh, duh, duh ..." I couldn't say his name. The air wouldn't come out.

I smacked the water with my rod, which agitated the venomous snakes more, swimming faster toward me. Suddenly, Dane saw the commotion, tossing his rod to the shore and clamoring over the rocks to pull me up out of the water; all the while, I held tight onto my rod. I began muttering his name repeatedly until he had me entirely up the slope of the dam.

I suddenly screamed and jumped onto my bike, clutching the rod – sadly, with a hooked bluegill dragging along the grass. I pedaled as fast as possible, but the adrenaline overtook me. I tried to stay on the path along the top of the dam, but my hands shook so fiercely that I lost control of my bike. I careened down the other side of the dam into the lake, now laughing uncontrollably at myself.

My brother followed me into the water, pulled me off the bike, and stood there laughing hysterically. We laughed so hard that our sides ached, and tears streamed down our faces.

Dane unhooked the bluegill and tossed it into the lake as we walked our bikes onto the top of the dam's road. Dane retrieved his fishing box and met up with me as I pedaled down the road, still shaking with laughter at my ridiculous reaction to the snakes.

He was my protector, and I loved him for that. He always watched out for me even when I didn't know it. Once, when we attended school, he always had his eye on me on the playground. The day he saw me punch Timothy Gothchild in the nose was a memory we would never forget without fits of laughter.

Timothy thought it was cool to make fun of me. For what reason, I have no recollection, but it got my gander up, and he didn't realize I rough-housed with my brother daily.

So, when Timothy said some choice words toward me, I jumped down from the monkey bars and let him have my full fist to his nose. My punch knocked him to the ground, leaving him twisting in pain. Dane was there in a flash, standing over Timothy, ready to swipe the next blow. Timothy got up and limped away in shame. I felt like the superheroes we watched on TV, the ones who wore magical rings on their finger to turn them into their magical power. I felt invincible with Dane by my side.

It was harder for him, however, to protect me from my sister and mother's torment. He'd try to stand up for me, telling my mother and father the truth of the accusations made against me by my sister, but it was brushed aside. Even though he was considered the 'golden child' who could do no wrong in my parents' eyes, my sister would plague them with false stories until she got her way, and Dane and I would suffer.

They never sought the details and banished me to my room or on my knees on the kitchen floor to face the wall for hours until one of our parents forgot about me or left the house for an errand or something. Then, I would go seek out Dane.

I could tell he felt defeated and maybe a little guilty. He would play with me with a game of my choice or take me on a bike ride. He was like the marigold protecting the tomato plant from the tomato worms that can infest a garden. Dane tried to protect me. However, there was only one of him and three against me.

Dane and I never fought. We made fun of each other but never fought or held grudges against each other. I could never hold a grudge against him since I wasn't built like that. If we caught the other with an attitude, all it took was a well-placed comment that would double us over in fits of laughter, which was the extent of the disagreement. I didn't realize what a blessing it was to have someone to be completely honest and free with. We knew we had each other's best interests at heart, and nothing would end our bond. It was an innocent belief I still long for today.

Dane learned how to hunt from our Uncle Armand. He was a helicopter pilot in the Army and had incredulous stories to go with his Hulk-like physique. We all admired him, especially Dane, who learned to dress a deer, clean a shotgun, and set up a deer stand.

One weekend at our parents' garden shop, Dane wanted to scout for deer. We had eleven acres of land surrounded by neighboring corn fields. I followed Dane to the west side of the property, where old ash trees grew to separate the properties. He had set up a tree stand the weekend before, so he scurried up the tree and got set. He had instructed me to walk along the south end of the corn rows and flush out the deer that had bedded down for the night. We knew they were there from the fresh tracks they had left in the dark dirt on the south end of the field.

I walked away down the side of the field and took about a hundred paces inside the browning tall wall of wilted corn. I could hear rustling ahead of me, but I couldn't see the deer. I wasn't sure if they were heading north or moving closer to my brother. So, out of curiosity, I walked east down the row of corn toward him. I reached the end of the row to see my brother picking up his rifle and aiming it toward a buck. The buck had no idea what was about to happen. Suddenly, I lunged forward and shook my arms wildly above my head. The deer took off into the field unscathed. I looked up to see my brother looking at me incredulously. He climbed down the tree and walked over to me.

"I just couldn't watch! I had no idea I would do that, but I just couldn't watch him get shot. What if he had babies?"

My brother's camo-painted face broke into laughter. I thought he'd be mad at me, but we laughed at how stupid I looked, scaring away his quarry. I promised him I would allow him the shot next time.

Laughing was our constant; he knew how to make me laugh instantly. We have so many memories that could bring us to tears to this day. That could also explain one of the reasons why my sister held such animosity toward me.

On one of those days when my sister bullied her way into our happiness, I decided I had had enough. I was ten at the time and decided to run away. I packed a wicker suitcase with my stuffed Koala bear, a few apples, a small fishing knife, and some gum. With my lack of provisions, I think I had planned to find a family to take me in and set off toward the creek down the road.

The creek ran through the neighborhood, meandering through the backyards of the homes across the street. Each house had an acre of land, and most let the blackberry bushes and small maple trees take over, providing excellent cover along the creek's edge.

I was gone for about four hours, enjoying the birds flitting in the trees and figuring out how far to walk that night, when I heard a rustle in the bushes behind me. My brother's voice sounded concerned when he spotted me, but then, as usual, he laughed his head off.

"So, how far did you think you'd get?" he asked, taking my wicker suitcase from me and shaking its contents. Then he walked back toward the street.

"I dunno. I figured I'd ask someone to take me in like the Czerniakowskis and let me do chores to earn my keep," I said matter-of-factly. "They understand how bad it was for us with our parents."

"Yeah, well, that wouldn't last long."

"But Dane, it's so bad back there. They always believe her. I don't do those things she says I do! I'm tired of it," I said, pointing back home.

He stopped in his tracks, understanding my plight. He didn't get picked on by our sister like I did, and Mom and Dad always believed her instead of me. I could see on his face the unfairness of it all.

He put his hand on my shoulder and walked me down a deer path toward the road. "I know. I don't get it. They let Sable get away with murder, and I'm sick of it, too. But we have to catch her in the act, and they'll have to see."

I shrugged, realizing it would never change, though we always seemed to pray it would.

Middle school was not exactly memorable, except I saw Dane in the halls with his friends. He'd whisper a funny thing to me, and I'd laugh, then search for a group of friends in the large lobby area splattered with couches and tables.

On the weekends, if we were allowed to go to work later in the morning at the family business, we would seek out his friends in the neighborhood. They'd make bike jumps or action movies with one of his friend's new video cameras. After a while of their antics, I would walk in the forest to look for owl pellets and broken pottery from the settlers that had lived there eons before.

When we got to high school, things became a little strained. Dane was striving for autonomy and needed to stretch his wings without his twin around. He also liked some of my friends, which made him feel awkward in their presence. I was also interested in some boys but never let it out of the bag. I preferred it that way since the knowledge of who I liked could be used against me. I didn't want the teasing to get out of hand, so I admired the boys from afar.

Dane joined the track team, and I managed the baseball and basketball teams, so our times together were shortening. Then college applications went out, and for the first time in our eighteen years of living together, we parted ways to begin our lives separately.

I missed my constant companion. We could go for months without talking and pick up where we left off as if there was no time or distance between us. On rare occasions, we would see each other during summer breaks, and he would share his dating world, and I would share mine. I compared most young men to him, realizing whomever I ended up with must make me feel loved and protected and, most of all, make me laugh.

Dane also used our relationship as a compass to compare the girls he was dating. He'd ask me if certain behaviors were acceptable in the women he dated. Some were so far from who I was that I couldn't relate to their trite and immature behaviors.

"Are you crazy? Unless she's got a good reason for behaving like that, I'd kick her to the curb. You deserve someone who sees the good in you and respects you."

It was plain and simple. We understood that most people didn't have a twin as their best friend and as their measuring stick.

Dane was respectful, kind, funny, and intelligent, but something about the girls he picked missed the mark. I felt the influence of our sister and mother had developed Dane's woman-picker, and I think it was broken.

None of the women he dated knew what an incredible catch he was. Years later, it was a chance encounter with a mutual high-school friend who revealed she regretted not accepting Dane's offer to date right after graduation. I had always wanted to share this with him since I knew he never quite felt worthy after her rejection. She was his ideal and unobtainable. This news could have changed his feelings about himself.

She was one of our graduating class beauties with an incredible heart. She was kind to everyone and always had a smile on her face. Years later, she ran into Dane when he moved home with his family. She was gobsmacked at who he became: a high-ranking pilot in the military with three beautiful girls.

But it was more than that. She spoke remorsefully. She had met a guy only weeks before Dane got the nerve to ask her out after high school graduation. She decided to give the other guy a chance, and later, he became her 'starter marriage.' She shared that she still regrets that one choice she made so many years ago. She knew if she had picked Dane, her life would have turned out differently, most likely for the better. However, there are too many lessons in each choice we make to know the alternative outcomes.

I longed to tell Dane that our friend wished she had chosen him. I have always wondered what he would be like if he had married her and if he would still be a part of my life as my loving and protective twin. I realized then the influence of our mother and sister's controlling ways embedded into his 'picker' of women. He would find someone who would control every aspect of his life and force him to let go of his twin sister due to jealousy of our unconditional love for each other.

This brings me to the other man in my life: my father. Most girls look up to their fathers as their guiding posts to measure their future relationships. However, as with my mother, I lost the hero complex toward my father during my early years.

Although my father was a gentle man who loved making people laugh, I couldn't get him to stand up for me to save my life. I could yell and scream at all of the injustices that my mother and sister would wage against me, and he would shrug his shoulders and step back. I could never understand how he would wane from conflict even though great travesties were occurring against me.

The struggles I suffered didn't leave bruises or marks. It went much deeper than that. Emotional abuse sets out vines of pain deep into one's Soul and can choke out any sense of love or familial connection. I wasn't beaten, but I was beaten down. It was a constant way of living, and over eighteen years of it can impact a person's sense of self and the world.

The times that my father barked back at my mother were often met with more screaming from her. He'd drop his hands and walk away. I slumped upstairs dejectedly to my room, where I would be grounded for days.

If my travesties were deserved, I would be admitting that now. However, it was the fact that Dane and I didn't do any of the things our sister accused us of. Dad was just the prison guard for the prosecutor, and our mother lashed out her punishment.

He would come and visit me when Mom was busy. He'd lay on my bed and talk.

"I understand what you're saying, Debbie and I know your mother may be taking it all out of context, but just lay low for now."

"But Dad, if you know she's wrong, why don't you say something?" I pleaded. I needed him to be my champion, someone who could right the wrongs and pull the weeds that choked my everyday existence.

But my father didn't carry a spade. He appeased my mother by agreeing with her, yet not going so far as to punish me himself. If he saw me kneeling against the wall, he would peek around the corner to see where Mom had gone and then tell me a joke. I'd fake a pathetic laugh, shifting my knees on the hard tile.

"Dad, it's not funny," I'd say meekly. "Why can't you tell her that Sable did it, and that Dane and I are being honest with her?"

"Well, you know it has to be your mother's idea. If I tell her how she should run this ship, all Hell may break loose!"

He'd stay for a few minutes longer. I could see the worry knit between his brows, looking sincerely sorry for my and Dane's plight, but he wasn't willing to go against his wife. To this day, I can't fathom giving someone else so much power to rule over others unjustly and allowing a child to overpower another parent. It was then I realized they were both afraid of Sable's powers over them. I still don't know what those specific powers were, except parents often fear their children's retaliation when reprimanded, and my sister had a way of demeaning their intellect. Sable was manipulative and smart.

The dynamics of my family were often affected by my father's tendency to allow himself to be kowtowed to his wife. This was particularly challenging for the rest of us, as we frequently felt that our needs and opinions were not being heard. Upon reflection, I realized that my father's Swedish upbringing played an important role in shaping his meek stance. His parents were strict and demanded that their children only speak when spoken to. This upbringing likely contributed to my father's stoicism, which lacked the nurturing he needed to grow in confidence and stand against the injustices in the world.

It seems he was bred to endure the pain and hardships without displaying feelings or complaints, a common trait among those who grow up in stoic households. However, this approach often comes at a cost, as it can lead to a lack of emotional connection and communication with loved ones. I hope that in a future life, my father will find a balance between his stoicism and his need to connect with his family.

I decided this was a family legacy I was willing to break.

Incompatible plants

Plant incompatibility refers to the inability of certain plant species to coexist in close proximity to one another. This can be due to various reasons, including but not limited to different water and nutrient needs, different root systems, or different preferred growing conditions. When

two incompatible plants are forced to grow close together, one or both plants may suffer from reduced growth, vigor, or even death. In some cases, incompatible plants may also produce harmful chemicals to the other plant.

CHAPTER FOUR

Identifying Toxic Plants

THE DARK SIDE OF SIBLING ABUSE

Wicked sisters do exist. I say this with love. The idea of a sister should bring a feeling of closeness and friendship and fond memories without the need for rivalry and judgment. Yes, sisters can be competitive, and rivalries exist, but even competing sisters return to the fold of sisterhood and protection. A sense of symbiosis occurs in families where siblings are taught to support each other's individualism and learn the benefits of being a cohesive familial unit, helping each other to thrive. This was not the case for my family.

When planning for a family, it is always assumed the children will get along, much like when designing the perfect garden. You go about planting the seeds, watching them germinate, only to find out they might compete for nutrients, sunlight, or water. The gardener's lack of knowledge and experience hindered the growth. The garden you thought would be luxurious with greenery turns into a pile of starving plants overwhelmed with plight.

What happens when that dream of the perfect family is impacted by poor parenting or a skewed view of how it should be done?

How often has it been said over the millennia that there are no instructions for raising children?

Seeds come to fruition with a complete genetic code to grow. However, many genetic codes can be wrought with variants, like being born predisposed to addiction, anger, impulsivity, or mental illness.

So what can a farmer do? They can nurture their crops, providing daily care to bring out the best for a complete and wholesome harvest. However, there is *only so much* a farmer can do until they decide to toss in the spade and start over with fallow ground.

Of course, we can't do that with our children. We can only nurture our children with care and love and then watch them grow into the people they are meant to become. Only then can we hope they will find their way along their path.

Parents, like farmers, only know what they know. A farmer with a sense of sustainability and permaculture can reap the benefits of symbiotic plant and animal relationships, which benefit each other. However, if a parent doesn't understand healthy relationships or how to nurture appropriately, they can wreak havoc on the children in their care. Sadly, those children will repeat the pattern set in motion decades and even generations later.

Since my birth, I have loved my sister deeply. Even today, my love for her remains, but with time, I have learned an important lesson about creating boundaries with people who don't show mutual respect or compassion or deserve my sincere love. That was the role she played in my life, and I respected that. We all need a teacher to show us what we need to learn.

I see her beauty, her intelligence, her strengths and weaknesses. This is the only way to grasp what our relationship was all about. If I look at her with only one type of critical lens, it is similar to only using one kind of gardening method to grow roses, neglecting that roses need specific nutrients and pruning patterns to grow and bloom. I needed to understand the makings of my sister, as well as what influenced her in her life, to be able to appreciate who she was to become in my life. She was the teacher, I was the student. Once the lessons were learned, I had to let her go. Then, it was up to her to embrace her new role and stand on equal ground with me.

My first memories of my sister were much hazier. I do not recall a sister who swaddled, protected or stood up for me when I needed a champion, as a sister should. Although I could remember when we played civilly together, I could not sense her as a loving entity in my earliest years. There was a reason for this, though I wouldn't recognize it until years later, and its impact on me as a young adult. We were products of birth order, but there was a nurturing trait my sister lacked for me. She seemed to have utter disdain instead.

Immediately after my brother and I were born, my sister had to take on the role of 'helper' to our mother since balancing the needs of twins meant double duty. My sister was two years old, and I learned through reflection years later how her idyllic childhood must have changed drastically.

Being an only child for her first two years and then waiting for attention while the twins were cared for was a lot for a toddler. I don't think it was ever addressed in her younger years. It was something expected from the older sibling with no recourse or complaint.

My mother would talk of times when my sister would help her feed us bottles or change our clothes like baby dolls. She would show us the old black and white photos, yellowing on the edges, as if to prove Sable loved me.

"You need to love your little brother and sister," our mother would often say as if trying to make the impossible happen with my sister and me. There wasn't that natural bond between us that my twin and I had.

I would stare at the photos of us twins cradled in each of my sister's arms. We were her new dolls, fresh from the hospital. She wore thick cat-eye glasses, and her wavy hair was pulled up into a half ponytail – pulled too tight. She wasn't smiling gleefully but more apprehensively, as if to say, "How long do I have to hold them, Mommy?" or "These are mine, Mommy, and I will do what I want with them."

At the beginning of our time together, she may have felt ownership over us. The attention from being the one to make choices for these new beings in her life meant she was important. But that didn't translate into protector, cheerleader, or nurturer as the years progressed. I think, inevitably, she was given that choice in this lifetime, but she chose power over nurturing love.

Over the years, the rest of the photos show Sable towering over me with contempt and power. The times my mother dressed us in the same dresses were photos of her disparagement of having to be similar to me. She wasn't gleefully loving the idea of dressing like twin sisters. I recall how I was told to stand or how she didn't want me in the photo in the first place. I see now, as an adult, that she only tolerated this little girl beneath her.

Some memories of my sister were of emotional or physical pain, buried under decades of protection I created so I wouldn't live in fear or self-loathing.

The first summer I came home from college, my mother asked me to get a blanket from the cedar-lined closet at the end of our hallway upstairs, next to my sister's room. I stood in front of the door, recalling an immense fear I used to have of this closet, but I couldn't place the reason behind it. I shrugged it off as silly childhood boogeymen and opened the door.

The smell instantly hit me. It smelled of the same earthy cedarwood that brought back floods of memories of feelings and emotions. It was unsettling, causing tingles to go up my spine.

Piles of thick blankets stacked several feet high still filled the hollow space in the middle of the floor. There was no path around them, so to reach anything hanging in the closet, you had to climb over the massive pile of blankets to get them.

My mother's elegant gowns and fur coats hung tightly on the left-hand side of the closet, sprinkled with my father's suits in old cellophane dry cleaner bags, opaque from years of abandon. A sizable wooden bureau cabinet sat along the far back wall with stacks of other items too cluttered to make out.

In the middle, hanging directly above the immense pile of blankets, was a lonely string attached to a single lightbulb on the ceiling. It hung about five feet off the ground, and I could not reach it. Since the blankets filled all sides of the closet, I grabbed the first blanket on top and slammed the door shut.

Chills went up my spine, though I couldn't recollect where it stemmed from. I laughed at my need to close the door tight and rush downstairs, wondering what could have caused such a chilling sensation through me.

Decades later, I had a chance encounter with a clairvoyant who told me what had happened to me in that small space. At first, I thought she was crazy until the woman went into further detail. It would take several moments to fully remember the incident with my sister. I couldn't believe what my mind suppressed all these years. I stopped the woman and told her the rest of what happened to me in that close space.

I was four years old. I remember my brother was not with me. I also knew my mother was out of the house, busying herself in one of her gardens, so I was alone with my sister upstairs. My father worked in the city, so he wouldn't be home until sunset.

It was a simple act of hatred or jealousy, I'm not sure which. My sister shoved me into the closet and locked the door. I heard her run downstairs, leaving me alone in the musty-smelling space with no light. It was completely dark. I tried to grab the doorknob, but my little hands would slip off the large knob. The hanging dresses and suits brushed against me, making crackling noises from the enclosed cellophane.

Pinned between the pile of blankets and the door, I could not move. My eyes searched for the slightest sense of light, but the blankets covered the bottom slit of the door.

I scooted backward to get on top of the blankets, but they would slide like sand on a dune under my weight. Suddenly, unable to get a proper footing, I fell into my father's suits, sucking the cellophane bags deep into my mouth. I gasped for air, only to have another bag waft into my mouth, causing me to panic more. I couldn't breathe. Each breath was blocked by another plastic bag, stopping my lungs from taking a full inhale. I remember seeing stars, causing me to fall deeper against the wall under the hanging garments. The harder I tried to breathe, the deeper the plastic went into my mouth.

My hands were bracing me from toppling over, so at one point, I had to release a hand which caused me to turn almost upside down against the wall, the plastic still sucking into my mouth. I wiggled enough to fall to the side, releasing the cellophane's tension suffocating me. I lay there for a moment, scared of taking another deep breath. I turned over and went on all fours, as best I could, with barely any room to maneuver through the long skirts of heavy organza and satin.

I desperately grabbed a blanket only to have it tumble on top of me. They were my father's heavy woolen blankets commissioned from the Naval Academy and weighed too much for me to push aside.

I planted my feet against the floor and wall, pushing myself free, and tried to climb the mountain of blankets again and grab the light string. However, the blankets unfolded, causing me to slide down and tumble into the suffocating dresses, pinning me against the wall again. This time, I turned myself on all fours, keeping my head away from the plastic garment bags. I followed the wall to the door and crawled up the blankets, facing the door. I propped my feet against the door to steady myself in that crouched position. I stayed like that for what seemed like hours.

I remember shaking with fear, but tears didn't come. I banged on the door, though no one was near enough to hear me. Sable must have distracted my brother outside, so he couldn't rescue me. I stopped banging and sat between the blankets and the door, listening for any sound of someone in the house. No one came.

Suddenly, there was the familiar creak on our staircase's landing, followed by the lock's simple click. The door opened, and there Sable stood in silhouette, my eyes blinded by the sunset shining in the hallway behind her.

From what I recall, I didn't say anything to her. I ran past her, blinking hard from the harsh light in my eyes. I looked desperately around her for my brother. I pushed past her and ran down the stairs as if my life depended on it. I found Dane outside near the shed our father was building on his days off, playing with his trucks.

"Why didn't you look for me?" I said to him, exasperated.

"What do you mean? Sable said you were sleeping," he said, pushing a fire engine up the shed's newly poured cement ramp.

"She locked me in the closet," I said, crossing my arms. "I was so scared."

"Why didn't you yell or something," he said, standing up to see my face reddened.

"I did, over and over, and no one came."

He stood there, unsure how to comfort me when our mother drove up the driveway. Dane put his truck inside the shed and raced me to the house. It was then I realized it was hopeless to fight this situation I was in.

I felt overwhelmed by this feeling that my sister was someone I could never trust to keep me safe and protected. It was my first experience of someone wishing me ill-will. Did she know the extent of what she was doing and the possible outcome that could have occurred? No. It wasn't that simple. She just wanted power over me. I would never look at her the same way again.

I never spoke to her about why she did what she did. I figured she wanted me gone.

It impacted me into adulthood, the sensation of being suffocated. I've learned to keep calm in hot spaces with no fresh air or watching someone lose their breath on television.

Ironically, there would be a second time, much later in my childhood, when my lungs stopped working, my breath left me again, and my only memory of my sister was of her looking at me in my hospital bed and then walking out of the room.

Sadly, I grew up wanting her to love me. I was desperate to have an older sister like the ones in the movies and television—the kind that would share secrets, go on trips with each other, and protect each other from mean girls. That was not the case, but I still loved and admired her.

She was brilliant, with long, wavy hair the color of caramel in the sunshine. Her body was petite yet solid and limber, as evidenced by the ballet and swimming lessons we took.

I always found her reading in her perfect room with the perfect lavender floral comforter, lacy pillows, and perfectly decorated bookshelves with books perfectly placed in order of the date read. However, there were cracks in that perfection I would learn about later.

On the other hand, my room was a flowery mess of live plants decorating my dresser and shelves. My bed was hidden under the multitude of stuffed animals with uncreative names like Pete the penguin or Koala the koala bear. My walls were covered with cheeky posters of kittens meowing, *Hang In There*, and the dry humor of Garfield comics.

It's not that I didn't appreciate fine things. I could not convince my parents to decorate my room to my liking as Sable did.

Two twin beds cluttered my bedroom for years until Dane moved into his room. Mom moved a tall old display shelf from the family's nursery and florist shop, which took up most of the wall. It was cluttered with empty cookie tins and holiday florals that Mom was storing for 'just in case.' A quilt from my grandmother covered my bed, but I wouldn't say it was my style.

Sable's specialty was throwing fits of displeasure, being the "Prima Donna," as my father would often mutter under his breath. I appreciated having my room, though I missed the late-night giggle fits with my twin.

Growing up with my sister was odd since she put off an air of her being of higher stature. Not only by how she treated me but also by giving the impression that she felt she belonged to a more affluent family and not a member of ours. It took years for Dane and me to piece together the sources of this grandiose behavior that always seemed to clash with the reality of our family's financial situation and status. Hints of it were introduced to me as a young girl, but it didn't come to fruition until I was old enough to understand family dynamics and ancestry.

Sable learned that my father's side of the family was very wealthy, and she was determined to find that wealth one way or another despite her middle-class family in our middle-class home. Sable let the world know that she was not a part of us, and she would make it known we were not of her kind every chance she had.

Mimicry:

Mimicry involves the evolved resemblance of a species acting as 'mimic' to a living or non-living 'model,' such that another plant or animal is

'duped,' unable to distinguish between them, — to the benefit of the mimic. Mimicry in plants is very useful for the plant's survival against herbivores and helps aid in pollination.

CHAPTER FIVE

Cultivating Understanding and Reflection

THE FARMER'S PERSPECTIVE

I t is so easy to find faults in others. Call it a natural human trait or a pastime of the idle; it reveals more about the observer than their subject. It makes the observer appear negative and unhappy but can also create tension and breed resentment. It can also cause one to feel defeatist, as though they are not good enough.

But what if we all took a step back to understand why people do what they do?

This is much like the farmer observing the weather's impact on their crops or the brand of seeds or fertilizer used in planting. The farmer scrutinizes with reflection, concluding with a better understanding of the dynamics affecting the growth of his crops.

Although I can look back at when I behaved as a little sister would when being picked upon, I can also remember trying to figure out why my sister acted as she did. We all have quirks and mannerisms that may cause some to question our character. There are many reasons for those *quirks* in a person's character, and getting to their root fascinates me.

Diving into the 'why' of why a person does what they do helps to reveal their humanity. We are all here trying to do our best with the little we were given to guide us along the way. When you can sit back and watch someone and then discern their reasonings, you become a more compassionate and understanding observer with no need to point out the obvious but comprehend that the person is on their *own* path to discovery.

Throughout my life, I have encountered numerous instances where women have caused me harm. However, instead of holding onto resentment or bitterness towards them, I have taken the time to understand why they acted the way they did. It's rather fascinating, to say the least.

This does not mean that their behavior towards me was acceptable or excusable. Instead, by gaining a new perspective and insight into our shared human condition, I have seen more clearly that we are all here to learn hard life lessons. This knowledge helped me move forward in a more positive direction, free from any lingering negativity or anger toward those who have hurt me.

The behaviors of these women stemmed from a place of dis-ease with their standing in life. They suffered from childhood abuse, alcoholism, depression, and severe enabling personalities with codependencies. Once I realized where they were coming from, I could step back and become the observer, choosing not to get entwined in their story.

My sister experienced a disassociation from her upbringing, which caused her to create a false identity for herself. This coping mechanism greatly impacted her perception of the world and her place within it. She struggled to connect with her surroundings and people and often felt like an outsider. The constant effort to maintain her facade took a toll on her mental health, and she found it difficult to express her true feelings and emotions.

We were raised in a musical household from my mother's love of the piano and singing.

The baby grand piano sat in the corner of the living room where my mother would amaze us with classical pieces like Malaguena, Ave Maria, Beethoven, Mozart, and even the show tunes of Irving Berlin, Bing Crosby, Nat King Cole, and Camelot. My fondest memories were standing around the piano and singing Christmas carols or sitting on the couch and listening to my mother play.

This is when my mother was at her best. She sat proudly on the piano stool as her fingers danced along the keys. Her voice was like an opera singer performing the show tunes, as my father accompanied her. His voice was in perfect pitch, and his eyes smiled during these moments of peace in his family.

The three of us would watch our parents put on a show, a semblance of normalcy, their voices in unison with each other. My father would turn the sheet music, and my mother would press the accent pedals on the floor of the piano's pedestal, her fingers knowing their exact placement. She played with passion and grit, the music wafting through the house like a cleansing of all the old negative energies. If only these times could be bottled and released during the lowest times in our home. We three siblings wished it lasted forever.

My mother learned to play the piano from the Preservation of Mary Nuns at Saint John's Catholic Dioceses in Providence, Rhode Island. At a young age, the children would learn piano from the Nuns, practicing an hour a day and then as homework after school.

Music was part of the family tradition. My mother's great aunt, Rose Marie Therese LeBrun, was a violin virtuoso, which influenced my mother's desire to learn the Violin. Still, it was too expensive at the time to acquire another instrument, so she played the piano.

My mother became quite good and was asked to perform at a competition at a local radio station, WJAR. She was sixteen and had to perform several pieces, competing with other students. She won several rounds until there were two students left.

She sat on the bench, smoothing out her blue crinoline-filled dress. Her black hair was pinned on the sides with wavy curls cascading to her shoulders. She resembled a young Jacklyn Kennedy wearing the latest color, though it took her months working at the drugstore to buy the dress for the occasion.

My mother won the competition and received a silver cup engraved with the sponsor's name. It sat in a glass-front cabinet in the living room, surrounded by my late grandfather's Swedish Orrefors crystal glasses and decanter. It was a memory of when my mother sought what made her happy.

Over the years, I wondered if my mother had kept up with her piano playing and performing, would it have given her the confidence to become the woman she was meant to be? She had a high school diploma and was a hard worker. Her mind worked differently than others, preferring asymmetry to things in order. This is reflected in all aspects of her being. But music put her on a level playing field, where she soared.

Our living room became the music room. My French Horn took over the side chair, Dane's saxophone propped in its case, and Sable's Clarinet gathered dust on the floor. When we turned twelve, Sable moved on to the Violin after completing our piano lessons.

My French horn was boisterous, booming through the house during audition time. I originally wanted to play the flute, but our teacher handed out the last flute during our fourth-grade music class, and the French horn was the only instrument left. Dane stuck with the saxophone during the required 5th-grade music classes and some time in middle school. I decided to go further with my music, enjoying the pieces we played in which I excelled.

Music came naturally to me. I auditioned for the Bucks County Youth Orchestra and made it into our prestigious Bucks County Symphony Orchestra as First Chair. I went to the auditions with headphones on and my WalkMan hooked to my belt. Ironically, I didn't know how to read musical notes very well, but I did play by ear, to my music teacher's surprise.

Luckily, the judges faced away from the auditioner, so when I entered the room, I put my sheet music on the stand and quietly clicked on the Walkman. The music would play in my headset, and I would follow along with the tape.

I was so happy in my element playing the music of Mozart, Strauss, and Tchaikovsky, though my favorite was playing John Williams' pieces like Star Wars and Indiana Jones. The French horn was the star, and I was in my glory.

I would learn what was necessary to perform well in the Symphony from our instructor, but I preferred to play with friends in the orchestra during our breaks. I would get goosebumps when the harmony resounded within our bodies when I played. The horn helped remind me that I was good enough and talented enough. It still holds a special place in my heart.

There was something about Sable, though I couldn't put my finger on it. Music didn't come naturally, though she could hold a pitch and sing well. Her desire to be exact almost stunted her ability to express herself naturally. Years later, it hit me why Sable could never quite perfect certain things. I saw it play out decades later when teaching my students about animal mimicry.

The lesson was about insects and how they can mimic the look of plants to thwart predators or attract prey. When one of my students wrote a report about a strange vine in Southern Chile, it occurred to me that my sister was like this vine.

A botanist was exploring the local flora on a walk in the hills when he came upon a plant with another attached to it. The second plant mimicked the same leaf shape as the host plant. This vine, called Boquila trifoliolata, would mimic the exact shape of the leaves it would climb upon. Whichever plant it mounted on, the B. trifoliolata's leaves would change shape. It did this to camouflage itself into the leaves of the host plant, in a sense, taking on its characteristics. However, the B. trifoliolata could not change to the original plant's colors or produce the exact flowers or berries during the change of seasons, giving it away.

This was my sister. Sable wanted to become whatever she could to escape the ordinary life of the Chapman family. However, something always seemed to give her away in the brightest of sunlight.

She squeaked on her reed with the Clarinet, and the strings to her Violin strained under her need to perfect it. Although she was more fluent on the piano, it was the Violin she wanted to master.

She had heard our mother speak of Great Aunt Rose Marie coming into ownership of a famous Stradivarius Violin called Bruno years ago. The facts are still a mystery, but it was plausible since Rose Marie was so deft at the Violin. This was enough for Sable to want to learn as well. To have an ancestor part of this elite group of violinists, playing a world-famous Italian collector's item was enough to spur Sable on. There was also the fact that my mother always wanted to learn the Violin, so there may have been a bit of one-upmanship involved.

There was a *je ne sais quoi* about playing a violin. It was Sable's desire for *perfection* that kept her from obtaining mastery of it, though.

The Violin strained because of her need to exact the right note quickly. It lacked the heartfelt emotion needed to make the instrument sing. She couldn't connect her heart to her music, which showed terribly.

Her desperate demand for perfection was shown by dressing a certain way or speaking with an affluent accent. Nevertheless, the Violin revealed her true identity – a wannabe so desperate to be seen as better than the rest of us. Like the B. Trifoliolata, she could never quite master the flower or the color of whatever she tried to imitate.

I had hoped for her to develop the ability to connect with her vulnerable side and demonstrate the real emotions needed to transform all areas of her life. Her prize would have been the power of owning her true self and identity. I picture her with a story of success, coming from a middle-class family, proud of her roots and hardships, and coming into her own as a successful woman humbled by her beginnings. But she was determined to become someone else and strap herself to the next influential host plant.

Our home was built in a colonial style, with a large brick hearth in the family room and a heavy wooden mantel over the fireplace. Wooden beams stretched along the room, reminiscent of the regional colonial architecture. It had four bedrooms upstairs, a separate kitchen and dining room, a family room, and an enclosed patio downstairs.

When it was built, the colors were muted and elegant. Each formal room, the living room, and the dining room had heavy brocade curtains in white, blue, or red and brown, respectively. The dining room china cabinet was filled with Waterford crystal glasses and vases, Nachtmann crystal wine goblets and pitchers, and sterling silver serving platters. The items were mainly from my father's side of the family, and wedding gifts were from his parents.

These elegant morsels were locked away only to be used during special occasions. They represented my father's potential in wealth, which I feel my mother must have noticed immediately when visiting her fiancé's family home in Chappaqua, New York.

They had met on a blind date when my father was heading home on leave from the United States Naval Academy. His friend from the Academy was driving to his girlfriend's home in Rhode Island and said he had a single female friend he thought my father should meet.

My mother and he dated only three months before my father went on his Southern Antarctica expedition with the Navy. During that time, my mother planned their future.

My grandfather's home in Chappaqua showcased opulent items of crystal glassware, fine china, and sterling silver platters that were not put away for special occasions but were used for everyday functions.

My grandfather, George Chapman, was born in Göteborg, Sweden, and moved to Stockholm to study. In 1924, he immigrated to the United States and founded the *Electrolux Corp* vacuum and appliance company in America and Canada.

As Chairman of the Board, Chief Executive Officer, President, and Treasurer, his office was in Manhattan. He had built a small empire for himself over the 40 years in his position. Electrolux thrived, and my father and his half-brother, George Robert Chapman, or as we called him, Uncle Bob, worked under their father to learn the family business. Uncle Bob did very well, learning the ropes and eventually moving on to run one of the largest advertising agencies in the world, *Backer, Spielvogel, and Bates,* for twenty years. Uncle Bob and my grandfather were part of the Fortune 500; sadly, my father was not.

We would receive company swag as gifts for Christmas from Uncle Bob. Gold bracelets with the imprint of the *Miller High Life* logo on it, a metal gold ruler with the agency's name engraved, *Beer On Tap Shampoo* samplers, and other products they advertised. We would get excited when we would see one of Uncle's advertisements on TV. Uncle Bob would also send us the mixed tapes of the advertisement jingles from *Miller High Life* commercials, *Campbell Soup*, and *M&M Mars* candy. When I hear those old jingles, it brings back memories of happier Christmases.

My father prepared to take over the South-Eastern regional offices for Electrolux and moved to Doylestown, Pennsylvania, once my mother and he were married. Sadly, my grandfather changed his mind about opening a South-Eastern office, and my father decided to find work elsewhere. This was most likely my father's decision, instead of staying with Electrolux, thinking he could do better elsewhere.

He became the Financial Analyst for American Motor Corp in the early 70s when we were all in Elementary school.

Dad would dress in his suit and leave before sunrise to catch the train out of Doylestown into New York City, returning to the house when the sun had set. He worked there for a few years until he discovered something wrong with the accounting system. Someone in AMC was *cooking the books*, as he put it. He decided that although he would likely lose his job, he had to report it to the FTC.

We were ten years old when the FBI came to the house. Dane and I stood in the kitchen watching several men in dark suits tape a wire onto my father's chest and put a device in his coat pocket. Dad made jokes about James Bond, trying to alleviate the tension in the room.

The agents spoke of the afternoon meeting and what they needed to capture on the tape recorder. We were mesmerized by these men and their calm demeanor. Doylestown didn't seem like the typical town the FBI would visit.

Dane seemed more worried about the situation than me. At first, he was excited, but then I could see his mind working out the dangers that could occur if my father's whistleblower status was discovered. Two agents watched over us kids for the next week.

We were dying to tell our friends but were strictly forbidden to talk about what was happening with our father. Dane and I would meet on the playground and watch the black Lincoln parked in front of the school's office, the agents reading and smoking while on watch.

A week passed, and the Agents gathered in the kitchen each night for coffee, reviewing notes and filing reports. My father got the crook to talk, and they were indicted for financial fraud. My father worked a little longer for AMC until the company's decline. A year later, the FBI rewarded him, eventually taking the family to Cancun with the proceeds.

This event, however, caused my father to rethink his purpose in life. He now had to decide whether to work for another company or create a business for himself. I saw the concern on his face. There was something about my father that seemed always to miss the mark when it came to business success. He was born with a silver spoon, but it was tarnished.

My father was born into a family with a maid, a cook, and a groundskeeper. His family's home was just down the road from Rockefeller's stables. He often rode to the stables and mingled with the oil tycoon's family.

His family belonged to the Mount Kisco Country Club in New York, which offered all that country clubs could offer. He golfed with his father and brother and attended the club's events. He dressed in trousers and buttoned-up shirts and knew the rules expected of all members. Trousers and button-up shirts remained his uniform for the rest of his life.

We heard stories of his swimming at the pool and the dances he attended and often wondered what it would have been like to have been part of such a club.

Grandfather George drove a Mercedes, accustomed to the finer things in life. He was stoic in the Swedish way, and we only spoke to him when spoken to, but I regarded him with great admiration at such a young age.

Grandmother Katherine, as she preferred to be called, was Grandfather's second wife. Uncle Bob's mother died twenty-seven days after he was born. Twelve months later, George married Katherine and had my father a year later, in 1935.

I feel this position in my father's life impacted him throughout his life. He felt second best, not quite filling his brother's shoes and wanting his father's love and respect. Grandfather was a businessman and needed someone to watch over his first newborn son, Robert. Although I feel he loved Katherine, a divide seemed present in the home, and there was preferential treatment toward the older son.

I also wondered if my grandmother's depressed mental state in her later years was brought on by her need to feel worthy and loved by George, as my father did.

Though I know the brothers loved each other, there was a sense my father felt slighted as a young man. Uncle Bob was given a Mercedes, and my father was given a much smaller car.

I gathered that it was most likely Uncle Bob's way with people. He was tailored and dignified, yet personable and worldly. My father was also personable and loved to tell jokes at every opportunity, but there was a need, a desperation to show he was worthy of a higher stature. I realized Sable and our father were cut from the same cloth, wanting and needing something intangible, which affected how they approached most things in life.

I was too young to understand most of my father's rivalry with his brother or his relationship with his father. However, I could see that my father's goal in life was to prove his father wrong; he deserved a great and successful life through his own efforts.

My dad contemplated purchasing a booming fast-food restaurant in Los Angeles. He saw the potential in this restaurant with Golden Arches, but for some reason, he backed out of owning the franchise. We heard of this deal years later and raised our voices in shock, understanding where we could have been financially as a family if he had taken that risk. Maybe it was my mother not wanting to move or not wanting to uproot his children from their schools. I want to think it was for a greater purpose.

We were silenced and scolded for our disappointment. Our discontent came from the fact that every day after school and on weekends, from age eight to eighteen, we were expected to work at our parent's new business, a nursery and florist shop. This was mandatory. We were paid .25 cents an hour, which didn't change over the ten years we were employed.

We were grateful for our home, food, and clothes but realized we were missing out on something more significant: a childhood. This wouldn't become apparent until we were out on our own, creating relationships with people still connected with childhood friends. Their tales of their antics seemed so foreign to me. It was like they all lived a TV-created life that I couldn't relate to, but I wanted to create when I was finally on my own.

My only childhood memories are of outings with my brother or time spent with Shawn and his family, as I never had a long-standing group of friends.

Hearing stories of how other children lived made me realize that our childhood was the product of two parents living in different eras. We understood as children that we were expected to work to help the family, save money, and not hire workers to take care of the property. We didn't know seven-year-olds shouldn't be operating ride-on lawnmowers and push-mowers. We weren't aware that driving a Kubota front-end loader tractor to dig ditches and ponds was odd. We knew how to answer customer's questions, answer phone orders, and help conduct business at age eight. It was just what was expected of us, and we took it upon ourselves to get the work done that needed to be done.

The genesis of our parents' new business came from my mother's interest in propagating flowers in our glass greenhouse attached to our home. My dad had built it as a hobby for my mother until she came up with the idea to sell her plants in the local grocery stores. Clemens Grocery Stores let my mother sell her houseplants at three locations, and Greenery Sales officially opened. This was when my mother shined in her glory amongst her plants and eventually showed her creativity in floral design.

My father decided to make a go of it and open up a more extensive nursery and flower shop, naming it Chapman's Nursery and Florist. My mother went to school in the evenings and weekends for Floral Design, eventually becoming a Master Gardener.

They would buy an eleven-acre parcel of land in Buckingham, Pennsylvania, off Mechanicsville Road. The nursery and florist shop was the closest to ranching since the flowers, plants, and trees needed constant tending. Every day after school, we were picked up to work the fields and incessantly weed pots inside the three massive greenhouses.

The eleven acres of land was our playground, and we had each other as playmates between breaks from working. Dane and I created adventures climbing trees and hiking around the pine-laden property. When Dane hunted pheasants, he would use me to flush out the birds from the tall grasses that covered much of the acreage. The birds would fly up, and I would drop to the ground, waiting for the shot.

On days our parents had to work late, the three of us would get dropped off at home, and we would cook dinner for ourselves and get to our homework. I learned to fry cod fish and egg foo young at eight years old, delighting in this freedom to create. King's Chicken Pot Pie and Spaghettios were always a once-a-week meal, but cooking from scratch was my favorite thing to do.

In the summertime, the drive to work each morning was beautiful, with pastoral views of stone barns and stone houses that stood since the time of George Washington and his troops. People took pride in preserving the region's history, and I felt blessed to live in such a beautiful place.

Doylestown was a quaint town on the eastern side of Pennsylvania, bringing to mind the countryside of England, with its rolling green hills, winding narrow roads canopied by great maples and oaks, and misty dells with horses and cows grazing lazily. I only knew of England's pastoral beauty from the large books that engulfed our coffee table in the living room until years later when I traveled there. The comparison was accurate, and I could see why so many of our founding Fathers settled in the region. It reminded them of home.

The Lenape Indians first settled in the area, then eventually founded by William Doyle in 1745 to build the famous William Doyle's Tavern that still sits proudly in downtown

Doylestown. Most of the original mansions stand as a testimony to the care of the historical society keeping history alive.

The drive up the hill to The Shrine of Our Lady of Czestochowa was picturesque. We climbed steep, narrow roads that meandered alongside creeks and small ponds draped in weeping willow trees or mossy rock outcroppings. I always appreciated the depth of green; if you stared at it long enough, your skin and eyes would soak in the green.

The charming countryside was dotted with mostly dairy farms, separated by rich, tall forests. We were lucky enough to be surrounded by virgin forests, where wildlife was abundant. Herds of deer stirred bouquets of pheasants through our yard, and our bird feeders were ripe with every East Coast bird species.

Our yard blended in with the forest that surrounded our colonial home. The two acres had various hedges, vegetable gardens, and orchards, depending on what tickled my mother's fancy that season. Although my mother loved her gardens, they were quite cumbersome, and the hobby became more of a battle with overgrown Virginia creepers that could hide pretty gladiolas and frolicking cement frogs within a few weeks.

One of my many chores was weeding these plots. I loved finding a piece of garden decoration covered in dense wild ivy. It was like discovering an ancient artifact hidden by time.

We were the only home in our neighborhood until after I was born. Then, approximately fifteen houses were built spread out from each other, all with the traditional colonial façade of either brick, stone, or white siding with black shutters framing each window.

The homes were elegant, keeping in touch with the New England charm of the region. Bankers, lawyers, and doctors lived in these homes. Old money was apparent in their cars, demeanor, and dress. Though our neighborhood was friendly, you could always pick out the Old money homes versus the middle-income homes, and we were one of them.

Our yard stuck out like a sore thumb. With my mother's love of gardening, the weeds took over every part of the yard. We three kids had to keep up with the yard work, which would become our weekend chores after working at the shop all week. We could never quite make our home look as lovely as our neighbor's homes. Three young children trying desperately to keep up with the manicured lawns and perfectly decorated landscapes was overwhelming at the ages of seven and nine. We were like the Clampetts living amongst the refined, which showed terribly as we spread pine needles or tired mulch around our trees.

This was the beginning of my sister's claim to wealth. She often joked that she was a Rockefeller and adopted by my parents. Dane and I would take full advantage of this aura she held about herself and fully teased her at every opportunity, to her annoyance.

Although my father's family rubbed elbows with these wealthy elites, he could not recreate it as his father and brother had. He always came close to it but then fell short. He tasted the life of Camelot, yet Camelot was only a distant memory of the posh life he once lived.

His early life experiences did influence us as his children, though. He wanted us to understand all aspects of socializing with folks from every walk of life, primarily the *well-to-do.*

So, at an early age, he showed us how to sail on our SunFish sailboat, golf with all its etiquette and rules, horseback ride, shoot archery, ski downhill, ice skate, and understand the delicate nuances of wine. We learned to Waltz and dance the Foxtrot, prepared for any social event. It helped us appreciate the art of conversation and eye contact.

We felt confident in all social graces, learning etiquette around the table and in all social situations. Practicing at church or when our parents would have holiday parties was mandatory. Learning these social graces helped us children become better accepted, especially when our parents lost all semblance of decorum. We could at least excuse ourselves or make pleasantries when our parents created an unpleasant scene, hopefully separating us from them when things got bad.

"We are one of you," we felt. "Don't judge us children by our parents' poor behavior," seemed a mantra we whispered to each other. These were the times the three of us siblings would bond, showing the world we were worthy of being loved and accepted despite our parents' behavior in the latter years.

Our father would take us to watch the America's Cup in Newport, Rhode Island, during our two-week summer vacations in Cape Cod. Watching the boats and the who's-who by the City By The Sea kept our heads on a swivel and in awe at the finer things money could bring.

Champagne brunches and walking among the elegant vintage cars of the Concours d'Elegance on the front lawn of The Breaker's mansion made our eyes pop! This is when I fell in love with vintage cars and desired a French roadster. My brother just nodded, amazed that we were simultaneously seeing the best in boat racing and car extraordinaire.

Sable looked like she was practicing walking with a book on her head, desperate to show she belonged with these people. Her New England accent was practiced and thick, and

Dane and I were sure to point it out every time she used it to her chagrin, reminding her she was one of us.

Our father would slowly drive us by the famous mansions of the Gilded Age, still in all their splendor. We would roll down the station wagon's windows and drool over The Breakers, Château sur Mer, and Vanderbilt's Marble House. Sable would purse her lips together and almost princess-wave at the people walking the sidewalks in front of these grand mansions. We would unabashedly mimic her, unable to comprehend her need to pretend at sixteen.

I am thankful for these memories. Even though we didn't live among the rich, we were exposed to many incredible experiences that helped us relate to all sorts of people in every step of life. I appreciated what our parents could share since these were the exception and not the rule of our life as a family unit.

Uncle Bob was the true affluent one in the family. He graced us with his home in upper-state New York with our cousins and skiing trips at his ski chalet on Stratton Mountain and Mount Killington in Vermont.

Our cousins were gracious and downhome. We loved visiting them and the chance to live a moment in their existence with their sense of style, fineries, and experiences we would never know daily. It was also about their ability to act like a typical family.

Their home was clean and neat, unlike how our parents kept their home. Each room was styled with proper seating and the comforts of how a home should be. They didn't have stacks of magazines, random papers cluttering the table tops, or messy and unclean floors and bathrooms. It was truly remarkable to see how a well-to-do family lived.

The cousins addressed each other respectfully and bantered in a competitive but friendly manner, never once showing jealousy or disdain for the other. It was cathartic for me each time we spent with them.

My Uncle and aunt were involved in many charity events and traveled extensively for Pro-Amatures in tennis and golf. I followed Wimbledon Tennis and golf at The Rosemont for the Augusta National to get a chance to see my Uncle on the leaderboard competing in the Pro-Am tourney.

Watching our extended family from afar made everything seem possible. We had a chance, through hard work, to attain the same things they did. This helped us discern what money meant. It wasn't just a means but a way of life; it had to be shared, not squandered away.

Sadly, Sable lived in two different worlds — one of a middle-class family whose parents owned their own business, toiling away seven days a week. She would do everything she could to escape the menial labor at the shop.

She would begrudgingly do what was asked when coming to work. It never occurred to Dane and me to rebel and argue with our parents' work expectations. Sable, however, would moan and complain that she had homework to attend to, which my mother wouldn't understand. Sable knew this would get under my mother's skin, pointing out that she was meant for college, a place my mother wasn't lucky enough to attend. Ballet lessons, modeling classes, and music lessons would fill Sable's schedule instead.

Sable joined ballet after stories of our Aunt Florina being a Prima Ballerina in Europe. This, of course, spurred on Sable's desire to become just that, a Prima Ballerina due to her pedigree.

Years later, when I was in my forties, my mother explained that Florina was a wealthy neighbor of theirs and not a member of the family, which made me laugh. Sable had hoped that by having the lineage in her blood, she strived for things that were not necessarily her passions. The hope of becoming something would elevate her over us by surpassing the ordinary. I understand anyone having desires and dreams, but for Sable, it was wanting to be a part of something bigger or an association that could get her to that next level.

I joined her for several ballet lessons but learned quickly enough it wasn't for me. She would scold me during breaks about my knees not pointing outwards and instead facing forward. She must have forgotten the foundation of my legs at the beginning of my life.

I realized it was best for me to avoid my sister during competitive activities. It wasn't like she excelled at any of them. Her inability to wholeheartedly embrace her passions prevented her from mastering them. Later, I also recognized that her insecurities held her back, even though she desperately tried to conceal them, becoming too rigid and forced. She attempted to force perfection but missed the mark of having a natural ability.

Horseback riding was short-lived for her. Horses sense the rider's mood, and she was too uptight to relax enough to allow the horse to bond with her. It was sad to watch. Her frightened eyes shared too much of her feeling that she had no control over a half-ton animal.

This inability to relax and become one with the activity became apparent when she hurt herself skiing in the Poconos. Our father wanted to ensure we felt confident skiing with our cousins at Stratton that year, so we spent the day learning the sport's nuances.

Dane and I excelled and had a perfect day on the slopes, taking off from my father and sister, who were having less than fun.

He tried to show her how to lean on the uphill ski when she caught her edge and took off in the wrong direction. She panicked and went head over heels in a soft berm of snow. Dane and I looked back just in time to see her screeching and screaming abruptly. Her legs twisted as she yelled at our father as if he had committed an act of violence against her.

Her voice was shrill, and even then, it wasn't natural. It was tight and exacting. She couldn't lose control, even in pain, and just let herself cry naturally. I felt sorry for her at that moment, not just because she was hurting but because she couldn't show her authentic self, warts and all. It was as if she always felt a camera on her, and one missed cue meant failure.

Later that night, my father told our mother that Sable was too scared and nervous to let go and enjoy the slopes. She behaved like that in everything he taught us. She could never relax.

I never thought of her that way until he mentioned it, but it made sense. She was uptight, always seeking perfection, never quite achieving it. It eluded her, so she tried harder to portray greatness by emanating power over others. She would put everyone else down around her to take the spotlight off of her inadequacies. Unfortunately, I had believed her most of my young life, and it would take years to shed her beliefs of me from my psyche.

After college, she developed a love of cooking when she moved to California, exploring new recipes. She would measure perfectly and time things precisely, but the result of the dish would be lackluster. I would praise her efforts, although many results were disappointing. She would blame the directions and toss the plate out.

"Well, at least your friends aren't coming over tonight. I can try to eat it, but I might have to hold my nose!" I would tease. She would shove my arm with a smirk, toss the food into the garbage, or have her husband, Matt, eat the disaster. I appreciated these moments since they made her more real and approachable. Someone that didn't have all her shit together was more lovable because she was like the rest of us; a garden of wildflowers and happenstance. This is when I loved her most. Only small glimpses of her authentic self kept me wanting to stay connected to her. It was the possibilities that I hoped for and wanted.

As an adult, it was more straightforward between her and me. I developed my father's ability to add humor to any situation that needed lightening up, and she would roll her eyes at my silliness. It helped to diffuse the situation.

I would tell her to add a pinch or a dash more of an ingredient or taste the batter and see what she thought. It was that simple, but she lacked the ability just to let go and use her heart, not her mind, to measure things in her life. She had finally mastered some dishes that became her pride and joy.

Maybe it was age smoothing out the hard edges and Matt softening her need for control, like when vines finally take over an asphalt driveway, and its rigid edges crumble. She was chilling to the reality that life shouldn't be taken so seriously. I loved her more during those times of genuineness.

Reflecting on why my sister was the way she was toward me helped me see her as an individual. Our years together as children helped me learn that her need for power and control was based on childhood fears and inadequacies. Twins took away her control of the love she received from our parents. That need for love and control then emanated from every act of her being.

There was an intangible space in her heart that needed filling, yet she didn't know how to fill it except with something tangible she could take or purchase. Her need to have something for the sake of having it was an oxymoron of sorts. She had the money to purchase anything she wanted, but it was the thrill of obtaining something that wasn't hers that she migrated toward.

This was apparent when we were young. Shortly after the FBI visit, we walked around a nearby neighborhood when I pointed out a friend's home. She was reading the Nancy Drew series, so creating stories about mysteries excited her.

She took me by the hand and walked me down my friend's driveway. I questioned what she was doing. "Why are we going to Sarah's house?"

"Because," she said curtly. "I think there's something inside we need to see?"

"But we can't go inside," I said, getting nervous with each step.

"Don't you want to see if they have something we can take that they'll never know about?"

At that moment, I was genuinely scared. I had been duped into thinking she wanted to spend time with me, and now I was approaching a friend's home to steal something.

She pulled me around the back of the house, where the garage door was partially open. I knew Sarah had a cat, so leaving the garage doors open was common to let the cat come and go outside as it pleased.

Sable pushed me down and had me crawl under the door. She followed and began going through the cabinets they had in the garage. She moved toward their refrigerator against the wall and took a popsicle from the freezer. At this point, I began to feel sick.

It never occurred to me to ever walk into someone else's home unannounced and uninvited. Sable was in ecstasy.

She opened the interior door and snuck in the house Nancy Drew style, slinking around each corner. She pushed me down the hallway when we approached a partially opened bedroom door. She told me to go inside when I heard a sound. It was a small screech of a voice. In the dimly lit room, a pale woman sat up in bed. Her fair pink skin matched the pale pink comforter. I could tell she was not well, and I tried to think of something to say.

"I'm so sorry," I said, barely audible, and ran out of the room and down the hallway. I was desperate to leave, stumbling over furniture in the unlit rooms. I ran out the front door crying hysterically toward a neighbor standing on the corner of their property facing the house.

My knees were shaking terribly as I approached her in tears.

Between my sobs, I told them, "She... she made me go inside, and I didn't want to!"

The woman put her arm around my shoulder and pulled me into her as she watched my sister stroll out of the house as the police arrived.

At that point, I felt bile come up my throat and felt faint. I couldn't comprehend Sable's need to see what she could get away with. All this for a popsicle?

The police gave her a talking-to and most likely took pity on me with my constant sobbing. I remember the neighbor lady telling another woman that the older girl had better get her act together, forcing the little sister to do bad things. I wiped my tears, thanked the ladies for being so understanding, and then ran home.

I don't recall whether she got into trouble after that moment or if the cops ever said anything to our parents. I think I blacked out anything afterward since the trauma had been too much.

My friend Sarah never seemed to say anything much to me after that. I apologized, but the police may have told her family the extenuating circumstances behind the 'theft.' I was bullied into it; it seemed to be the consensus, and I agreed wholeheartedly.

Sable was like a shoplifter in life, taking little innocuous bits into her pockets, yet it never filled the void. She didn't understand what it would take to make her feel whole since vulnerability was too risky. Her desperate need to fill her heart with completeness was something unattainable. It would always stay out of reach until she faced her fear of being unlovable and loving herself instead.

By learning to accept and love herself, Sable could finally fill the void she had been trying to fill with material possessions. She would no longer need to be something she wasn't. This is what I hope for her, and maybe someday I'll get a chance to see it.

Prune:

Using pruning shears, scissors, a knife, or loppers to shape or rejuvenate a plant, not to increase branching. Generally, pruning is much more drastic than pinching. Over-pruning will accelerate the process of decline in a tree's health.

CHAPTER SIX

The Art of Pruning

It's odd when you meet your siblings as adults. I knew Dane would become a successful United States Air Force pilot and eventually settle down and have a family. Sable would carve out her niche in the legal world and find a partner who could love her the way she needed, making up for what she didn't receive from our parents. She chose not to have a family, which fit her requirement to ensure things would go as planned.

Although they both had climbed to the top of their careers, I could see the small imprint our childhood left behind. Dane held on to grudges too long, and Sable still needed to control every aspect of her life. I'm sure they could say I held onto something, though I have changed immensely since I was in their life.

My intuitiveness grew over the years. I could see and feel cues from people's missteps of behaviors and words. I could now sense even deeper into the intentions of others, which made me learn to create firmer boundaries when necessary.

Sable had tried to reconcile with me once I was out of college. She had moved across the country to California, where she had always wanted to live, and she had created a beautiful life there.

We stayed connected through phone calls. There was still a sense of authority over me when I shared issues about leaving Jack. I didn't take them personally, however, since I realized she had never gone through the phases of ending a marriage, especially with a child. Sable swore never to have children, so I knew she wouldn't quite understand the complexities.

I would visit her and Matt several times a year when I needed time to recharge, not only from teaching but from the stress from my marriage with Jack. There was a strange mixture of acceptance and walking on eggshells around this adult Sable. Although I was invited to her home, rules had to be followed, like putting things where they belonged and not letting the cats out of the house. All made sense, as any house guest would respect the rules. What was strange was witnessing Sable's awkwardness with her life.

She still kept lists, her birth order gleaming through—that need for precision and control. However, Matt seemed to love spontaneity a little more. It softened her persona when I saw her wilt slightly under Matt's assertions to relax. He was good for her.

It also helped when she had a glass or two of wine. That is when I saw a closer glimpse of the Sable, which I think more people would have fallen in love with. This Sable was more self-deprecating, funny, and laughed more freely. I believe that is what Matt saw, and maybe he tried to bring her to that brink on purpose to see Sable's potential to enjoy life, warts and all.

During my visits, I saw she didn't have it all together, a recognition that my childhood perceptions put her too much on a pedestal. I was surprised to see her house was similar to our mother's. Sable did have Matt's influence, so most things were put away. But her cleaning skills were like our mother's; dust bunnies crept across the floors, and dust veiled most unused surfaces. It struck me that her DNA was much like our mother's, though she would deny that if her life depended on it.

Dane pointed this out when the family visited her home for one year for Christmas. He walked around the house, and I followed him to her pool. He chuckled, looking at the spider webs around the sliding glass doors.

"I can't believe how much Sable is like Mom," he said, almost too much like a grand revelation.

"What do you mean?" I asked, following his gaze.

"Well, for one, all of those spider webs are black widows! It's just like back home!"

"It's not that bad," I said, surprised to hear Dane criticize Sable so easily.

"Why are you defending her? She is just like mom. Not only her poor housekeeping skills, but even in how she has to control everything at dinner, she did the whole counting out the slices of bread Matt had eaten."

I laughed. "Yes, though I liked how he grabbed two more pieces just to spite her. Why didn't we think of that when she had counted out our Oreo cookies?"

Dane shook his head, putting his hands on his hips. It was the first time I heard him as an adult confess how much he hated how she behaved toward us as kids.

"It was just so ridiculous, how she had to count out everything, like the world revolved around her. She expected everyone and everything to play by her rules. Pretty sad."

I looked over the pool toward the sunset. I agreed with Dane, and it was indeed a revelation to see how much Sable emulated our mother's control and judgmentalness even into adulthood.

"I guess it didn't hurt her too much. Look what she has now?"

Dane's wife, Tatiana, joined us at the pool. She must have seen my expression.

"So, are we talking dirt about Sable?" she said, sipping her wine. She leaned in closer as Dane put his arm around her.

She whispered between her teeth, "Matt didn't seem to like how Sable was divvying out the seafood tonight. You would have thought she was passing out the family heirlooms."

Dane pulled her close, "Tati, she hasn't changed one bit. This is what she was like to us, but ten times worse. She totally controlled our parents."

He looked back to see Sable and Matt talking with them in the kitchen. "Yeah, of course Mom and Dad only see their posh house, but man, she hasn't changed one bit. I can't believe Matt puts up with her shit of control!"

Tati patted him on his chest, "Not so loud, they'll hear you! And personally, I think she knows if she blows it with him, she'll be alone. Matt's the fun one."

I saw Dane is a new light then. I knew he hadn't visited our sister much, except for these family get-togethers. I was surprised about the grudge he held on to so tightly. I was able to compartmentalize my past with Sable, put it in a place for childhood memories, and chalk it all up to "everyone has a chance to grow and change."

I gave Sable the benefit of the doubt, so it was surprising to see Dane's emotions so heightened. It was then I realized Dane had a harder time letting go of the travesties that plagued our childhood. I wondered how much resentment he was holding on to that he should let go.

Matt and our dad walked out to the deck. "So glad all of you could make it this Christmas!" he said, raising his glass of wine.

We all clinked our glasses and watched Matt turn to us. "It really means a lot to me. As you know, losing my parents last year makes me appreciate family that much more."

We clink our glasses again. Tati winked at me as she sipped her wine. Dane raised an eyebrow, micro-expressions that said so much.

Matt walked Dad over to the garden. We sat on the patio, watching the last bits of sunlight behind the hill.

Dane lowered his voice, telling Tatiana, "Matt is such a good guy. He has put up with a lot, for sure."

Tati seemed comfortable dishing on the family. She already had run-ins with our parents during their wedding plans a year ago. Tati had earned some of her stances on the Chapmans since they caused a major issue during the planning of their special day.

I was unable to attend my brother's wedding due to being in the last stages of pregnancy with McKenzie and not allowed to fly across the country, so I was unable to watch the drama unfold. The sting of our parent's dysfunction on his special day still burned in Dane's heart.

I knew Dane's perspectives influenced her, too, so I couldn't blame Tati for agreeing.

Sable and Matt traveled the world, planning exotic trips on chartered sailboats, hiking in jungles, and witnessing the Pyramids— something I wasn't able to do on my meager teacher's income and having to raise McKenzie. It would someday be my reality, but for now, I would enjoy Sable and Matt's tales of faraway places.

Matt saw Sable and all her flaws, and that is what made him special. I am certain that Matt was told of our childhood antics from Sable's perspective, so his stance was naturally going to be different than ours. What was odd was Dane and I never really filled Matt in on what life was like with Sable. Maybe he was able to read between the lines, and I know he saw my trepidations when Sable reared her old self with me. But the past was the past, and I was willing to forge a new path with her as adults and hope my sister would want the same.

Dane shared several more stories with Tati as Matt and Sable showed our parents around their property. We stayed at the pool, reminiscing about the crazy Chapman family episodes of dysfunction.

Later in life, I witnessed Sable's childlike tendencies that persisted into adulthood. I was able to analyze her behavior objectively, and I realized that her actions resulted from her upbringing and personality. Due to her manipulative nature, I had to reevaluate my sisterly relationship with Sable, which was unhealthy for me.

An innocent phone call years later to my parents brought back memories of how detrimental their parenting was and how compelling Sable's control over my life as a little girl was. I called to inform them that McKenzie had been accepted into the Gifted and Talented program at school.

"Well, we aren't surprised," my dad exclaimed. "The apple doesn't fall far from the tree."

I laughed. "What do you mean, Dad?" thinking he was referring to himself.

"Deb, you were tested in elementary school and you scored in the 99th percentile in several areas."

"Wait, what?" I stammered. "I don't remember getting to attend the GT program."

Mom piped in since they were always on the speaker phone together. "Well, yes, Debbie. It was in third grade, and you scored high in several areas, like spatial and mechanical awareness."

"But why wasn't I in those classes, then?" I thought back to the kids returning to their regular classes with fascinating items like rocks and geodes from the Geology class and shark teeth from a visiting marine biologist.

I heard my father hem and haw for a moment. "We thought it was best to just put you in the fourth grade mixed classroom instead, you know. So you could be with the kids a grade older than you."

I was puzzled. "So, I was supposed to go to the GT program, but you didn't let me go?"

Dad paused, "Your sister was in the program, and she didn't want her little sister in the same program as her."

"Are you kidding me, Dad? You mean to tell me I was supposed to attend the GT program in elementary school, and it was Sable's choice to keep me out?"

Dad chuckled on the phone, "Well, you know what a Prima Donna she can be."

I countered the excuse. "You realize I am helping to revamp the GT program in our school district, so I am acutely aware of how these programs accelerate our GT students. It can offer so many opportunities that they can't get in typical classrooms. McKenzie can participate in internships, and graduate with AP credits toward college, as well as receive certifications."

There was silence on the other side of the phone.

"Wow," I said. "I guess I'm not shocked by anything I learn about Sable's influence on my upbringing."

Dad tried to lighten the mood, "You probably wouldn't have wanted to be in that class anyway, since it was mostly older kids and geeks anyway."

I chuckled, "It's a status symbol now, Dad, to be a geek."

Trying to help them understand the disservice they did so many years ago was useless. And really, what difference did it make?

Though I see it often now in teaching, downgrading a child's education for the sake of another child's "feelings" was absurd yet familiar. Instead, it could have been a valuable lesson for Sable to learn that everyone has the potential to do well and to applaud her little sister for a job well done. It wasn't the case. Teaching humility must have been a dying fad.

What would I have done differently if I had known I was bright? What would I have accomplished? How would I have thought about myself? I knew I was smart and had a knack for certain things, but my intelligence was never validated in a quantifiable way. I went by what I was told, mainly by Sable.

It was such an innocent conversation with my parents and became incredibly profound. Sable had the chance to be my champion, my cheerleader, and even then, she took her power and used it against me. She cut me down instead of cultivating my knowledge and allowing me to grow to my full potential.

I saw other families championing each other when there was time for adoration. The Teter and Czerniakowski families all rallied together to show support and accolades.

I pictured myself, later that evening, what it could have been like as that awkward, freckle-faced, green-eyed, strawberry-blonde girl knocking on the GT program's classroom door, my binder clasped in my arms.

I pictured the door opening and a gleam of sunlight pouring out from behind Mr. Shielder, the GT teacher, inviting me inside. The children would clap their hands as I entered the classroom, and a girl two years older than me would escort me to a table in the front of the room.

I would see my sister, her mouth agape, watching me walk to her table, setting my binder next to hers. Her jaw clenched and her fists folded, unable to complain to Mr. Schielder, standing directly in front of us.

"Welcome, Debbie," he would say, handing me a copy of the Greek tragedies. "We are so happy you could join us today."

I would sit grandly at the table and raise my hand to answer questions about Socrates, Physics, and String Theory while my sister would sit there, her arms folded in defeat.

I awoke from the daydream, wondering what life would have been like if she had no longer reigned over my life back then and how much further ahead I would have been in my journey now.

I sighed and realized I could not change what happened many years ago. I forgave my parents again for their lack of ability to parent with boundaries and authority with Sable. I also forgave myself, remembering all the times I would belittle myself, thinking I would never measure up to the yardstick that was Sable.

I sat with the information and let it sink in, replaying it in my mind, reaffirming that I was a smart little girl. No one could take that away from me, not even Sable. If anything, I felt sorry for her. To desire ill will on me, putting her needs first, revealed an even deeper story about Sable and her desperation to oppress anyone who made her feel less than perfect.

***

This wasn't the only time Sable manipulated my parents into making decisions that would impact me later. I recalled when I was younger and felt confident in my appearance. As a young girl, it never occurred to me to think any differently until my looks were instantly altered. The memory came back to me years later when I was in high school when I thought of how I was different from the other girls in my school. I tried to keep up with the styles and trends but preferred the elegant styles of my mother's era.

My fair, freckled face, green eyes, and blonde lashes made me blend in like a washed-out calico dress when a dear friend grabbed me into our high school bathroom and put mascara on me. Seeing my green eyes pop for the first time was life-changing, and other friends' reactions were encouraging.

Before the sun rose above the trees, I would wake up early to put on make-up and blow dry my Lady Diana haircut to avoid Sable's eye rolls. My mother would ignore Sable's remarks, though I had wished one of my parents would intervene. They felt she was jealous since I applied my make-up with a natural flare and I could style my hair well. They would ignore her teasing toward me.

Sable preferred to go natural, having olive skin, dark lashes, and hazel eyes that looked more gold than green. She didn't look like my brother, who had blue eyes, light skin, freckles, and red hair. My green eyes were the closest to hers, and I stood two inches taller than her. But my mottled, freckled skin and light hair were in such contrast to hers.

I wouldn't realize until I was a young woman that my sister lacked the talent to wear make-up and style her hair after seeing her at an event with almost orange lipstick. Her attempt at eyeshadow only brought her close-set eyes closer. It was probably best she went natural after all. However, if we had been close, I would have loved helping her bring out more of her natural beauty.

I longed for a sister who wanted to bring out my beauty and support me in helping me decide what to wear. But this would never be the case. I was very young when I realized my sister never wanted me as her equal in intellect or beauty but her inferior. My friends, however, showed me I could be beautiful, and they did it in a way that made me feel they cared. They didn't force me to wear make-up; they just showed me how it brought out my beauty— and the vague memory of my sister's control and jealousy came back to me.

Although I am reflecting now as an adult, I try to imagine the thoughts that must have gone through Sable's mind to want to cause harm to me, be it emotional or physical pain. It wasn't in me to manipulate or 'plan' an execution, so it was beyond me that Sable planned out the haircut. I was seven at the time.

She decided that my mother only had time to comb and pin up one of our heads of long, beautiful hair. So, it was determined that I would be the one to get a haircut. My mother couldn't stand Sable shrieking when she pulled the brush through her long, wavy locks. Sable didn't always brush it thoroughly so that knots would entangle, causing my mother to pull harder. It was my turn afterward, and I think my mother had lost all interest and patience by then, so Sable suggested we get haircuts.

When it was time to go to the barbers, I didn't quite comprehend what this meant for my self-perception. I was so young and didn't remember spending much time in front of the mirror, but I did love my long hair. It felt like a natural part of me.

I remember sitting in the barber's chair, perplexed as to why I had to be the one to get my haircut and not both of us. Sable brought up the latest movie with Mia Farrow, who played Peter Pan. I knew the movie she was referring to, but it didn't hit me that Farrow's hairstyle was a Pixie cut. The Pixie had made its rounds with celebrities, but I was just a young girl trying to figure out who I was, too young to notice.

The Pixie was named after the mythological Pixies, the Sprites that inhabited the forests. The hair was cropped short to the head, a little longer in the front, with short bangs.

It must have been quite a shock to see my long blonde tendrils slide down the black cape and fall to the floor because I don't recall this time well. I think I had gone into shock.

I remember my sister's face as she stood before me, watching the barber cut the last of my length. The barber faced me from the mirror so I couldn't see the devastation. When I looked up at my big sister, she had a strange Cheshire cat's grin, as if her master plan had worked.

When he turned me around in the chair, I saw my twin brother looking back at me. I no longer looked like me. I don't remember tears or crying. I think I was shocked that I was to look like a boy now—an unremarkable second boy in the family. I think back now at this defrocking of my beauty at my sister's hand.

There was no point in screaming or demanding the barber put it back. I accepted the deed as done and lived with layered, short hair throughout elementary school.

Sable grew out her hair below her shoulders and down her back. She would make fun of my bangs as often as possible by taking her hands and pushing them up and off my face, laughing at my exposed forehead.

I became acutely aware that I must look ugly without bangs and kept them most of my life. It's so strange how these sibling acts can impact you on a subconscious level. I knew where the perceptions came from, but it took a lot as an adult to shed those old beliefs.

She pruned away anything that might have been better than her, anything that was my strength.

Jealousy is a natural emotion for siblings, but it isn't a trait to ignore in our children. Ironically, jealousy is the third most common motive for murder. Let that sink in!

The green-eyed monster is a great lesson for the jealous child. Learning to discern their feelings about why they are jealous in the first place could have been a great way to address Sable's behavior toward her little sister.

Well-balanced adults understand that jealousy is an emotion based on insecurities. Of course, I know that now. But it would have been so satisfying back then to hear my parents tell Sable that jealousy against a sibling is unhealthy and have her confront these insecurities against her little sister. However, Sable was allowed to live in her created world of control and judgment without restitution.

I grew my hair a little longer by middle school, thankful that Dorothy Hamil and Princess Diana made short hair all the rage. For years, I was called Lady Di. It boosted my shattered ego by being referred to as this beautiful woman, even by proxy. I didn't grow my hair past my shoulders until I was in college, where I finally felt like myself again.

After the defrocking of my hair, I asked my parents if I could get pierced ears so the customers at the nursery and florist shop would stop calling me my twin brother's name. The little gold studs didn't help. So, I decided clothing could help me stand out as a girl.

I chose the Preppy look as my go-to style. I would wear my mother's charcoal red and green plaid pencil skirts that she wore back in school with a charcoal cardigan. I'd wear gloves and a scarf with my wool coat and match them with ballet flats to round out the classic look.

I loved dressing up for school, but always in a vintage style rather than following the trends. Trends cost money, so I stuck with what my mother had in her closet—the classics never go out of style. Lady Diana also inspired me to dress appropriately for any occasion.

Sable was enamored with Brooke Shields and Grace Kelly and often spoke with a New England accent when speaking with adults or when she was miffed with my naiveté. Her one-time getting light layers put into her hair was met with so much praise. However, she couldn't maintain Brooke Shields's look and grew it out with frustration.

Despite having the Lady Di haircut and being given the nickname, I remained true to my personality by being silly, snorting when laughing too hard, and goofing with my brother. On the other hand, Sable was more comfortable in impersonating Grace Kelly or Shields. She would try to walk like a model and use phrases such as "Oh, wouldn't you like to know?" or "Whatever do you mean?"

Dane and I would embarrass her by mocking her proper proclivities as she tried her best to make herself not part of the family. Dane and I would put one hand on our hips and the other in the air, sashaying around her when she'd put on airs. It was our way of knocking her down a few pegs and letting her know we knew the real Sable and that this one was fake.

I wish I had known then that Sable's behavior indicated her insecurities, which haunted her most of her life. If I had, I wouldn't have tried so hard to seek her approval because I felt confident when she wasn't around. I still craved her love and acceptance. Looking back, I realize this need for validation was harmful to me, and it wasn't healthy to let someone hold so much power over who I should be.

Ironically, pruning helps to rejuvenate a plant so it can focus on branching out or blossoming. Despite the efforts to cut me down so many years ago, I blossomed.

Teaching siblings to support each other is an essential aspect of family dynamics. When siblings learn to cooperate, communicate, and care for each other, they can create a positive and supportive environment that blossoms growth and development.

I can see now that my mother's need for her eldest daughter's help raising twins created suffocation and resentment in Sable, whether she knew it or not. What could have been a relationship based on mutual respect, trust, and autonomy turned into one filled with tension, frustration, and a constant power struggle.

Although the circumstances that led to this are unfortunate, it's important to recognize that underlying issues needed to be addressed for our relationship to flourish.

Soil Amendment

Soil amendments are anything added to soil to improve its abilities, including water retention and absorption. The goal of soil amendments is to provide a healthier environment for roots to grow.

CHAPTER SEVEN

Amending the soil

RECONCILIATION AND THE UNEXPECTED OBSTACLES OF CHOICE AND EXPECTATIONS

I never thought there would ever be a day when Sable would apologize to me. It was something my heart and Soul needed to hear for so long. It meant the world to me to listen to her admit what she did to me was hurtful and wrong. I was willing to forgive her for every misdeed and continue into a new relationship with my sister. Life, however, has strange ways of bringing new lessons and challenges.

The day of her apology was unexpected, though I could see from her demeanor that she had planned the whole conversation from where we went to lunch to the stroll along the quaint street afterward.

I remember each step we took and where we were at, like the recall a person has when thinking back at where they were when JFK was assassinated or the Towers fell. It was surreal.

I had just graduated from college and moved to Boulder, Colorado. I visited her and her husband in their home in San Diego. She took me on a walk around the quaint town of Del Mar after lunch and said she wanted to talk to me. She seemed nervous. We had been laughing at something our mother had done when we were children, feeling the mutual bond inmates must feel when recalling a similar fate. It was refreshing to see her let her hair down with me and share the truths of our childhood.

"This is something I've been wanting to say for a while now," she said, pausing and letting the laughter quell. I know I haven't been a good sister to you, and I want to apologize to you." Her words were soft, and tears were in her eyes.

I think she was afraid as well and was waiting for my response. I felt my mind halt with each word as if doubting what it was hearing. I played the words again in my mind. My heart leaped into my chest, realizing I was hearing the words I needed to hear for almost twenty-four years.

I could have grabbed and hugged her, but I was also afraid that too much emotion would cause her to balk and take back what she said. I remember saying it was okay, and I understood why she did what she did. At that moment, I had no idea why she hated me all those years, but the words were like a purging of hearts, a cleansing, allowing us to start again.

She mentioned a few times she had done me wrong, smaller travesties that most children went through. I knew this was her confession, but I felt she knew she had many injustices against me, and she would have had to repent. But I was not her confessor. She would have to come to terms with each mistreatment of me on her own.

I held on to that apology for many years. It helped me move on and accept that the things she did to me were in the past. I had also grown to understand her as a broken child, and she was trying to reconcile with what she had done in her life. This was her journey, not mine.

We tilled the soil, eliminating years of the rocks of anger and roots of lies. Fertilizer was added when she admitted doing things to get me into trouble, and I ended up laughing at all the memories we dredged up.

She didn't quite explain why she did those things. I think the little girl in her was still trying to figure that out. She feared I could retaliate with harsh words and accusations, but I forgave her. I wanted a sister, not an adversary.

We began calling each other once or twice weekly, sharing our week's events and recipes. It was a magical time for me, sharing the intimate aspects of daily life like sisters should.

I confided in her about my impending divorce. She was as supportive as possible, considering she didn't have any children, and didn't understand why I didn't leave McKenzie with her Dad.

Only a mother could understand that leaving McKenzie with her Dad was not an option.

We would talk almost every Sunday or during her commute home from work, and I would get a report on how one of us siblings was the "low man on the totem pole" by our mother.

Sable and I were usually neck and neck, considering she had lived with her husband before they got married, a mortal sin in our mother's Catholic eyes. I was the low man after McKenzie had her First Communion in the church and refused to have her take Confirmation classes when she was old enough to discern which religion she wanted to follow. By then, I didn't hold my mother's judgment to heart. She was set in her ways, and I wouldn't try to change them.

Sable spoke of how Dad was going off the deep end with End of Times prophecies. I told her he was feeling his mortality since it didn't bother me that he was searching for meaning in how the world was shaping up. She was uneasy by his Faith in Mother Mary and the Saints. She didn't believe in anything she couldn't see or touch that was concrete.

I'd tell her that Dad and Mom were a product of their beliefs and didn't need to impact how we felt about them.

"Well, I don't respect anyone that would follow anything so blindly," she said curtly.

"They are who they are, but it doesn't change how they gave us a home and our college education." I didn't see cutting all ties to them as necessary just because their beliefs didn't gel with mine. A farmer doesn't toss the fruit just because it's bruised.

Our conversations would move on to gardening, the latest trip she and her husband planned, or how her two new Maine Coone kittens were doing. I'd visit during my breaks for a few days while she worked, and I loved the freedom of enjoying the beach and time to myself.

She would plan a few outings where we would visit and talk, though I would see snippets of her old self arise on more than one occasion. If I put on makeup before going to a new restaurant, she would admonish me and my efforts to look nice, stating that most women in San Diego went without makeup. I'd shrug my shoulders and swipe some mascara on.

She would remark on what I would eat and poke at my rib cage, indicating the little weight I had gained. My hair color was almost always remarked upon, and I put up with it because I wanted to have a sister who wanted me near.

When McKenzie was old enough to enjoy her aunt and uncle, she would come with me to visit. Sable's husband, Matt, loved having McKenzie around to spoil. He considered himself a dinosaur since he was a single child, and his side of the family would soon be extinct since Sable refused to have any children of their own. McKenzie was closest to having a daughter, so Matt soaked it in.

During my visits, I enjoyed watching Matt assert himself against Sable's controlling behavior. Whenever he noticed her curt behavior, he would call her out on it. Seeing him rein her in was refreshing, and it gave me a sense of vindication, knowing that other people could see her need for control.

Sable and I could have become best friends after that, but this was short-lived. Our sisterly connection ended in 2015. Her need to overpower and manipulate me became too strong for even her to resist. She had met an ally in the family and realized she had someone to aid her in controlling the family's narrative about me, and my sister became my nemesis again.

Dad was dying of cancer. He had been fighting it for years due to the exposure of RoundUp from the ten-plus years working at the nursery and florist shop. He was able to fight it for many years until it came back with a vengeance.

When I took McKenzie to school in Boston, I decided to spend a week at home before dropping her off at Boston University. I asked Dad to share some stories I might not get to ask in the coming months, though he only shared the same memories about his father's time in Stockholm and my father's time in the Navy on his Antarctica expedition.

I could tell he wanted to say more to me. They hovered on the tip of his tongue, but the words just floated away. I think he was too afraid of the emotions that would follow if he apologized to me for years of not protecting his daughter.

I didn't hold it against him. I understood he was just a man on a journey of his own. His eyes filled with tears, but he kept a smile to ease any fear a daughter may have of him passing too soon.

The week I got the call that he had fallen and was in the hospital, I knew it was only a matter of days. We spoke several times, and I could hear his fear of his impending death, but there was also an acceptance that this was his time. I reminded him that Mother Mary would be there for him when he arrived home, and his many family and friends were waiting for him. He told me those words brought him solace in those last hours.

"I hope that is how it will be," he said, more lucid than he had been earlier that day. The morphine drip was taking him slowly away.

"You and Grandfather and all the uncles will be having a grand time catching up, golfing, sailing and cracking jokes, "I said, causing him to chuckle.

He spoke of how he found a rose petal in the pew at church one day that looked like a portrait of Mother Mary, and his great devotion to her had grown since then.

He asked me how long it would take to get home to see him. I told him I would speak to the nurse to let her know my travel plans. He handed the phone to his attending nurse, who was checking on his morphine levels.

"The earliest flight I can get on would be tomorrow from Boulder. With an almost four-hour flight and another hour on the train, barring any delays, I could get there tomorrow about nine at night," I told the nurse.

She paused, and I could hear her start and stop her thoughts, "I would never tell a family member not to come, however, I also understand the feelings of just missing their loved one after extensive traveling not to get there in time."

She paused again, stepping out of the room. "Debbie, the amount of morphine he is on now is keeping him comfortable. His organs are shutting down. It's only a matter of hours until they stop altogether."

Her words slowed down in my brain. This was it. He was leaving us very soon.

"It's alright," I told her. "I know you can't tell me either way, but I know that if I tried to get there and he passed..." I trailed off.

"Debbie, he's told me he doesn't want you to see him like this. I guess you're a special one to him, and he says he'd rather have you remember all of the grand times you two had than this being your last memory of him."

Her words caught in my throat. I knew this was the greatest gift he had ever given me. I wanted to hold on to our memories of our times together, laughing and singing together, not the shell of the man being left behind. I didn't want those pictures to be in my mind.

The nurse put him on the phone, and we spoke for a while, though I knew the morphine was causing hallucinations, bringing out his most significant fear of not being able to protect me from my sister-in-law and her father. It was odd that this worry pressed upon his last conversation with me.

"They will try to come after you, you know," he said, warning me of Tatiana and her parents.

"Dad, you don't have to worry about them. They know I had nothing to do with their startup company going bad -if they even bothered asking me what the company's lawyers said."

"But they aren't listening to what Tatiana did— she deserved to be fired," his voice heightened.

"It's okay, Dad. We really don't need to talk about this right now."

"I need to know you'll be okay."

"I'm fine. When Dane and Tati are ready to have a mature conversation about it, I'll tell them what they need to hear. The company was doomed to fail anyway since it invested in someone who was committing security fraud."

"Yes, but they aren't rational, Deb. They'll blame everyone else except themselves!" he said, concerned for my safety.

I knew he was slipping at this point. He continued.

"Your brother should know better than to think Tati was suitable for the job. She was a teacher's assistant in college, for Christ's sake. You were more qualified, and she was less than professional on that conference call they overheard." Dad seemed to get a second wind. "Two times, for that matter! That was very unprofessional of her," his voice sharpened. "She deserved to have been fired."

Where was this Dad when I needed him to stand up for me and tell Dane that his wife and parents were wrong?

"Well, she was fired for her behavior, Dad. I couldn't save her anymore. She demanded to be paid before the company even launched and was earning any profit. Sable even warned me and was glad I hadn't dropped everything and quit my job for the company."

Luckily, I was still teaching and didn't need the income. I believed that the company's dream of building laptops for underprivileged children in third-world countries was a worthy cause. My background in training teachers and having my National Boards was finally appreciated. However, the company's president and the lawyers said that once the startup's founder took the money for personal use, they would have to remove him from the board, and she went with him.

"You know honey... it's Dane I worry about..." he paused and took a long, slow breath. I could tell he wanted to get this off his shoulders. "He should listen to you and what you learned from the lawyers, but she's controlling everything he hears. He's your twin, and that means something, but she's obviously jealous."

Dad was right. Dane was too afraid to cross his wife and stand up for his twin, who did not need to lie or deceive them. His wife could sometimes be careless and volatile, but I chalked it up to her young age and possibly trying to save face since her attitude ultimately caused her to be fired from the company. I was the scapegoat.

Dad shifted in his bed. I heard the chiming of the morphine pump. "I'll tell Dane he needs to talk to you when I see him next week. Sable also needs to be put in her place. The lawyers told you specifically not to speak to her or her parents."

The morphine was digging its claws deeper. I could hear Dad take longer, slower breaths in and out, and I knew there would be no more 'next weeks' for him.

I wanted to steer the conversation on a more positive note, but I knew that my father had been burdened by his family situation for some time. The morphine had loosened his tongue, and I was grateful to hear that he would have defended me if he had the chance. It was also revealing. My father was afraid that his son was just like him -- a man who was too afraid to stand up to his wife's abusive behavior. They were both tragic characters in a story of cowardice and fear of confrontation.

In a sense, Dane *had* to move his loyalty to his wife—what's the old Bible saying about cleaving unto his wife? He had to protect the mother of his three daughters. I was an innocent bystander watching it unfold, and Dane had to keep his wife happy.

I also knew I couldn't fight it. I didn't find out that the company's founder had stolen thousands of dollars from his in-laws' angel funds until after Tati was fired. They thought I knew all along. It's funny how people don't ask questions because they fear the answers they'll hear.

Dane's wife created her downfall with the company without my help. Several times after conference calls, she would remain on the line with a barrage of insults toward the company's founder and president. I'd listen for a second, then let her know we should continue the conversation later. I'd text her to get off the conference call and call me later.

She was overheard twice defaming the men, and they were not impressed. The company's president called me several weeks later to offer me the lead position in training our clients. I was more than prepared for this leadership position since I had trained teachers district-wide for over six years. Her parents' angel funds were the only connection to Tatiana. She had also sent a scathing email about getting paid or else.

I called Sable and Matt one night when I had concerns that Tati's behavior would cause her trouble. They told me that startups were never a sure thing and that the game we had to play was patience. They supported me with the new startup. Sable knew that if I received a contract for the job, McKenzie and I could finally move out of Boulder and back to Pennsylvania. She also knew that a startup was risky and that it was good I was teaching and not risking all of my income for this new venture.

I kept Sable apprised of everything happening with this company and shared that I was worried Dane's wife would get fired for her behavior.

"Well, that's her fault if she doesn't know conference call etiquette. She *should* get fired."

"I don't think she'll get fired, but she's not impressing them, that's for sure," I said, pausing. "What if she got fired? Did this mean I had to quit, too? Sable, what if that does happen?"

Sable didn't even pause to consider. "That's her fault then, and you stay with the company!"

"But isn't there something wrong with me staying with them if she goes? She's family."

Sable laughed at my naïveté. "Of course not! She's too immature to notice that you don't behave like this when a company is choosing its employees. You have every right to stay with them. She also sent out that scathing email demanding money."

I sighed, "I told her not to send it, but the lawyers already took me off the company's email list, so she never got my reply email not to send it. Once it was done, what was I supposed to say?"

"The lawyers were most likely trying to find a paper trail of the communications," Sable said, since she was a lawyer herself.

"It was strange when I wasn't getting any updates on our projects. She didn't believe me when I said I had no access to the internal communications."

"Her immature attitude is what got her fired, so you shouldn't be afraid of her," she said.

"I'm not scared of Tati. I feel bad that I know how much she wants to have an income and a steady job — and her parent's money being lost. However, this job is perfect for McKenzie and I, though. McKenzie can travel with me since she's homeschooled."

"Exactly! She's just jealous of his twin. You know him better than anyone, and that would threaten any woman. And, besides, you're more qualified. You need to also remember what she did to you."

"What do you mean?"

"Debbie, she purposefully changed the date of their wedding so you couldn't go!"

I had completely forgotten about it. I was eight and a half months pregnant when Tati changed the wedding date, sooner rather than later. I was devastated not to be able to attend my brother's wedding, but I also knew I wouldn't risk the baby's health, so Jack went in my place as Dane's best man.

"I forgot about that. But that doesn't have anything to do with what is happening now."

"Tati didn't want you bringing the first grandbaby to the wedding and show her up. You know that's why she changed the date. She doesn't care what happens to you. It's all about her, Debbie. I wouldn't protect her at all. She wouldn't have your back, and she's proven that to you!"

I always tried to make Tatiana feel comfortable and included in our family. Their marriage brought out our mother's wrath, which caused a lot of fuss and unnecessary stress while planning their special day. I always felt terrible for Dane that our parents caused such a rift during a time in his life he should have been celebrating.

Furthermore, I enjoyed my phone conversations with Tati, during which we talked at length about her daughters or the latest condemnation of my mother. I did worry, though, that Tati was bad-mouthing Dane in front of his daughters while he was away flying. It wasn't his fault his career took him away from his children. He was protecting his country, which was all the information his children needed to know, not "Daddy is missing your birthday, or Daddy won't see your play."

Sable never seemed to like Dane's choice of wife, often remarking about her control over Dane and her Catholic dogmatic behavior during family gatherings. I understood Sable's opinion, but I was willing to overlook his wife's behavior to maintain a relationship with my twin brother and his three daughters. Despite Tati's occasional poor behavior, I remembered her many beautiful traits.

I treasured my nieces. I visited them more often, learning about each one's personality. I saw Dane in each of them, which made my heart so happy for my brother. I could tell they loved it when their father's twin would visit them and share stories about our childhood adventures. I also saw myself in each and realized how much we were alike. I was excited about being a part of their lives and seeing them grow into the women they were meant to become under Dane's guidance. He was a good father and gave them the love and attention he wanted as a child.

I shared their antics with Sable. She was childless, so I never thought she would feel jealous of their love for me. However, when the opportunity came, she couldn't resist. She allied herself with Dane's wife against me when the whole company debacle happened. Instead of Sable defending my position with the company, she created lies. All she had to do was tell Tati and Dane the truth, and the conversation of maligning me would have stopped.

I don't know all the details except when his wife was fired for her behavior. I called my sister and asked for advice. At that point, I didn't know about the security fraud case against the founder and the stolen family money yet; it was just that Tati was being let go.

Sable listened and told me to stick it out with the company since it meant McKenzie and I had freedom away from Jack and Boulder.

Two days after Tati was fired, the company's president, who would take over after the founder was indicted, called me. He explained that Tati was fired for her behavior and that they had to cut ties with anyone associated with the founder committing fraud. The president explained that the lawyers were trying to determine if any funds were left.

"We hope to sort it out in the next few days. Apparently, this is his second attempt at security fraud, but we will know more tomorrow," the president shared.

"Have you contacted her parents yet about the funds?" I asked, unsure of how fraud investigations work.

"No, not yet. We are worried about him running, and if they tip him off, we may never find any money left, and get access to the accounts." The president cleared his throat. "If you think she will keep quiet, then you can tell her about the ongoing investigation, but it's a risk. Do you trust her not to tell her parents?"

"I'm not sure she would be able to sit idle with the information. Once I tell her, I'd have to trust that she could hold it under her hat and not tell her parents who could tip off Philip."

"That is exactly what we don't need right now, so it may be in her family's best interest to just let it play out. Besides, there is nothing they can do. Thank you for your understanding, Debbie. We look forward to seeing this company get a fresh start soon."

Three days later, the company's founder was indicted for security fraud. I called my sister, but she didn't answer. I left a message on her phone.

She never called back. I called Dane, and it went through to the speaker in their car. His girls were playing in a soccer match, and the din of parents cheering on the sidelines filled my receiver.

A barrage of accusations followed. Dane and his wife were yelling about what I knew and why I didn't tell them. I calmly told her what the lawyers stated, yet she didn't want to hear it.

She screamed even louder, which solidified my choice of not telling her in the first place. She proved that she couldn't act calmly and responsibly with the news.

I was in my office at school when she went into a tirade. My students and teacher's aide could hear Tati on the phone. "Look, this isn't a good time to talk. I have student assessments going on. I can talk more later," I said, hoping to quell her rage.

The accusations didn't make sense. I was just the messenger, and I was being persecuted. They also didn't realize I had never dealt with fraud or legal matters like these, and was unsure of how it could all play out for the company if Tati tipped off Philip and he fled.

"I'm not sure why you think I had anything to do with you getting fired or your parents losing their money, but if you talk to the president and the lawyers, it will all make sense."

They hung up. That was pretty much the last time we ever spoke about it. Sable and they were against me, and to this day, they have created this enormous lie about what happened. It was out of my hands since they never asked me any questions. If they did, they would get the answers they didn't want to hear.

***

This was the purging of the weeds that filled my garden, choking out any semblance of normalcy in the family. The soil was forever tainted, and there was no going back to the same plot of land. I had to let them all go and decide how I wanted them in my life on my terms.

It was almost laughable that I was Tati's scapegoat instead of her having to face the fact that her less-than-professional behavior was why she was fired. Regarding her parents' investment in someone who stole their money, angel investing was always risky.

As for blaming me? This seems to be a reoccurring default when people do not want to face themselves in the mirror and take responsibility for their actions and choices. It is laughable now. I've gotten used to this knee-jerk reaction from those who don't want to see the truth.

They get into sticky situations, and I'm usually there to help them or maybe take the stinger out and point them in the direction of clarity. Then all hell breaks loose for them, and I am the one they blame for their offense.

I often wonder why it's so hard for people to reflect on what they have created. It's playground behavior when wanting to point the finger at someone else instead of realizing they have four other fingers pointing right back at them.

There was no amending this garden of lies they created. They fed each other the stories they needed to hear, fortifying them with weeds of ego mixed with invisible pestilence of shame and immaturity. The roots they created dug deep, further into the furrows of denial and self-importance.

So, even though Sable did apologize to me for the less-than-lovable childhood she shaped for us as sisters, her words now lay in a compost heap decaying in the sunlight of truth. She was incapable of starting over with me, her true self shining through again. She could have finally been my champion, but her need for power overtook any chance of a blossoming relationship with me.

I was stronger for the lessons I learned. Although we were given titles like sister, brother, twin, or spouse, each of us creates a human expectation of the role that person plays for us. When that expectation isn't met, we find ourselves disappointed.

What if the roles we assign to others set us up for failure? As parents, we expect them to nurture, protect and guide us. But if they fall short, should we suffer the consequences? Perhaps we should remember that parents are humans, too, and they are also learning along with us. Children can learn valuable skills from less-than-perfect parents, such as resilience, patience, humility, fortitude, and faith. The list goes on.

In our lives, we often encounter situations where we have certain expectations from the people around us. For instance, we expect our spouse to be loving, faithful, and protective or our friends to be trustworthy, reliable, and supportive. However, we feel disappointed, hurt, and even betrayed when these expectations are unmet. We may even question the relationship and the intentions of those who failed to meet our expectations.

We must recognize that our expectations can often be unrealistic and one-sided. We all have flaws and limitations, and expecting others to be perfect is unrealistic and unfair.

Our struggles and disappointments in relationships may often stem from unrealistic expectations we place on the people around us. Communicating our expectations clearly and being open to understanding others' limitations is essential. Doing so can build healthier and more fulfilling relationships based on mutual respect, understanding, and compassion.

By embracing my expectations of them with love, I was finally allowed to let go of all hurt, forgive myself for wanting them to play their perfect role, and set them free from my emotional landscape.

Maybe next time, I would have a sister who loved and supported me, a father who protected me, and a mother who nurtured me without judgment or control. It was okay. I came away with precious lessons and lots of compost to help feed the seeds I planted for my future.

Natural Instinct

A way of behaving, thinking, or feeling that is not learned: a natural desire or tendency that makes you want to act in a particular way. A lioness possesses a natural instinct to hunt.

CHAPTER EIGHT

The Children's Garden:

INSTINCTUAL GARDENING, OR HOW WE MESS UP OUR KIDS!

Parents are given perfect seeds to nurture and grow. Babies come into this world reaching for their parents' warmth, love, and attention no matter what garden they sprout from. In my twenty-five years as an educator, I've seen children grow up in homes without heat, food, love, and normalcy. I've seen the end-products of these parental farmers, and depending on the child's chaff, it will determine if they grow into hardy adults or whither into victimhood.

I must also share that I am a mother. Like all mothers, I only know what I know or have learned. However, I was determined not to repeat my mother's mistakes and to carry forward the good things she taught me. I have a passion for nature, birds, animals, alternative medicine, and all things French, to name a few. I don't believe in feeling guilty or conforming to societal expectations because of my mother's dogmatic religious influence. Furthermore, I genuinely believe that people can transform and develop themselves over time.

As a parent, it's always a mix of pride and worry to see your child go on their own journey of self-discovery. My daughter is currently exploring the world, and I cannot help but think of all the amazing experiences she'll have and the challenges she'll overcome. I know she'll see the world through a particular lens, but that lens will change and evolve as she gains new perspectives and insights.

It's like a farmer who learns new techniques or discovers ancient pearls of wisdom - we all change and grow over time. Even though I miss my daughter dearly, I send her my love and prayers every day that she'll stay safe, happy, and true to herself as she navigates the ups and downs of life.

Teachers are also facilitators of growth if they do their job correctly. We guide and steer our students in the direction of learning. We correct with deference and encourage taking risks to help them learn from their mistakes.

We are farmers, prepping the garden of their minds for a prosperous future. Of course, I would warn how important it is for parents to be involved in their children's education due to the current events in the world today- but that is for another day.

Over the twenty-five years, I have been in education, I have witnessed the impressionable minds of my students, and it surprises me each year that we hand our children over to a stranger for nine months at a time.

Although there are many natural-born teachers I had the privilege to train over the years, many more shouldn't be pressing their perceptions onto our future citizens. By this, I mean the most significant flaw I saw when training hundreds of teachers toward the end of my career was their constant need for absolutism in the classroom.

Many teachers believe that if they don't teach, the children will not learn. Ironically, studies have shown that teachers only represent 30% of what a child learns through their direct lectures. Children learn best by doing, not by being talked at.

Let's look at the animal kingdom as an example. Most of us can recall watching National Geographic specials and Mutual of Omaha's Wild Kingdom television shows from the early 60s to the late 80s. It has now reincarnated into Animal Planet on cable television.

These television shows demonstrate how nature is the ultimate teacher, and we should all take notes.

Watching the lioness raising her cubs in a perilous environment fraught with dangers lurking in every corner, we see the innate instincts given to her to teach her cubs as much as she knows before she must relinquish her role as protector.

We don't see her take out notes, lecturing all day long with her cubs watching her intently on their haunches. She grabs them by their scruff and demonstrates what they need to know about life on the Serengeti through experience and practice.

A cub's life is rife with risk. How does a mother lioness teach her cubs about predatory lions, hyenas, fire, and floods? Paws-on experience, of course!

When the cubs are old enough to leave their protected den, the mother takes them out for lessons about the world. She guides them through the paces of hiding from predators, finding water, and learning the cunning steps of approaching a kill.

None of this is done by wrapping them in bubble wrap. For their survival, they must learn by doing. Only when the lioness feels they are ready does she release them from her care. From that point, she must trust they learned what they could to survive independently.

Technically, we have our children in our care for eighteen years. That is a lot of time to give our children hands-on experiences to help nurture them into the people they are meant to become. Mind you, I said "who they are meant to become," not who *we* want them to become.

Over the twenty-five years I have been in academia, I have watched the variants of parenting styles that create exceptional children with great futures ahead of them. I have also seen the effects of poor parenting, even from well-meaning and loving parents. Children are impressionable, even into their late teens, and we send them off to college thinking there are only well-meaning adults to guide them. I think we all know now that isn't always the case.

I want to share with you what I have learned about the human version of Animal Planet —the things that have created strong, resilient children and the things that can cause them to become lesser versions of themselves- far from the people they were meant to become.

Tommy was given a mother who couldn't relinquish her fear of being in a loveless marriage. Her husband was a truck driver and was gone most of the time. She relied on her little eight-year-old son for attention and love, and this overgrown need was choking Tommy's autonomy.

He entered my classroom with a file that determined he had Obsessive-Compulsive Disorder. Many of my students had such acronyms after their names. Oppositional Defiant Disorder, Attention-Deficit Disorder, Attention-Deficit Hyperactivity Disorder, Autism, Turrets, Asperger and more. Some of these disorders are not caused by DNA or chemical exposure. Many of these are learned behaviors by planting seeds of fear or being exposed to an environment of unhealthy "soil."

Tommy sat down at his chosen seat and proceeded to wipe it down with antibacterial wipes his mother provided. (This was years before the pandemic.) The students next to him watched, then looked at me and my expression on how to measure the situation. I just observed quietly, smiled, and moved on with the lesson. The cubs were learning tolerance through my behavior.

I watched Tommy throughout our first week together and found a very fearful boy. He washed each pencil daily and laid them on the desk. This set him up for being in a classroom with eight and nine-year-olds; the need for perfection would be challenged at every corner. The Serengeti classroom can be a cruel place.

"Ms. Holmén! Ashley just moved my pencil!" Tommy screeched as I demonstrated how to read a schematic for a Kinector set at the engineering learning center.

I gave Ashley the 'look' that meant not to test the teacher, and she promptly returned the pencil. Tommy then made a grand gesture by taking his canister of wipes from his desk and washing down the offensive pencil.

The lioness's glare is all it should take- not incessant talking to Ashley and why she shouldn't take her classmate's pencil. I let it go to see how Tommy handled the grievance.

Interesting, I thought. How long had he been taught that the world was a place of fearful germs? Or was it more about controlling every part of his environment? Time would tell how much his mother's fears influenced Tommy.

I finally met Tommy's mother during an unexpected conference two months after he had been in my classroom.

Years prior, I had built a nature habitat between our two buildings with a waterfall that led into a pond, raised garden beds, birdhouses, and grassy areas to sit and observe nature's bounty around us- nature being an excellent teacher.

My students were the stewards of The Habitat, and each parent who requested me that year knew it would be a year full of adventures. They learned how to maintain the grounds, plant vegetables, and learn about vermicomposting with worms. Another teacher hatched Pekin ducks and Quail from eggs to raise in the Habitat. My "cubs' thrived getting out of the classroom and learning about real-world skills.

On one specific day, I was teaching my students science, the symbiotic relationship of water lilies, and how they provide oxygen to the fish in the pond. Each child was given a small lily plant to observe and note what they saw. Tina had forgotten her gloves, so I asked Tommy to share one of his gloves with her. Tina was a diminutive student with fair skin, white-blonde hair, and light blue eyes. She was so lithe a gust of wind could knock her out of step.

"Tommy, Tina needs to have a glove to hold the lily. Could you let her borrow one of yours?"

Tommy looked at me like I asked him to donate a kidney. He put both of his gloved hands behind his back.

"These are my gloves," he said defiantly.

Several children stood beside me, slipping off one of their gloves to let Tina borrow. I put up a hand and smiled at their generosity.

"Oh, all of you are so sweet to want to help Tina so quickly!" I cooed at them.

They felt my appreciation and stood by in case Tommy was less than generous.

I smiled at Tommy, understanding he didn't know this lioness's ways. "Tommy, all the students in my class have learned about altruism."

His eyebrows furrowed, "Well, I don't know what altruism means," he said, twisting his gloved hands behind his back.

"Oh, that's okay, Tommy. When we know we can do something good for someone else, we never know if we'll get something in return. It could be a hug or thank you. But we should give of ourselves without expecting anything in return. It's the giving that is the gift."

Chad, one of my former third-grade students and old Soul, jumped up to share what he had learned that year about altruism. "Yeah, it's awesome, Tommy. We had no idea we would meet the Air National Guard after Christmas. Ms. Holmén thought it would be nice to send them a huge box of things they might need in Afghanistan with cards we drew for them. Sure enough, at the end of the year, the Air Guard came to our classroom and surprised us with awesome military-type gifts, too!"

Several students shared their stories of altruism with Tommy, and I thought I saw a glimmer of hope, his wheels turning at what it all meant.

Tina put out her hand, hoping it sunk in and that she would receive at least one glove from Tommy. Tommy looked at her and said, "These are my gloves, and I don't share them with anyone."

Tina looked up at me, startled at the rebuttal. I hugged her as several students saw the opportunity and handed her several gloves. She smiled wide at the love and went off with a gloved hand to pull up a water lily with several other students. The cubs had learned well.

I moved Tommy to a bench in the Habitat and sat down with him. He took off his gloves and sat on them. I felt saddened for this unfortunate boy who was learning that the world was a fearful place and needed to control his possessions. I could see the other students were perplexed by his behaviors and steered clear of him when in group situations.

Eight and nine-year-olds do know the difference between right and wrong. Their prefrontal cortex and amygdala are connected enough to discern choices, so it wasn't that Tommy wasn't old enough to understand his choices could be detrimental in social situations.

This learned behavior would be challenging to break if it grew unchecked.

I expected to hear from Tommy's mother soon after, and I received a note in my office box stating that she was requesting a conference that week.

I shook her hand as she sat at the kidney-shaped table, her size overwhelming the child-size chair. Her weight alone told me she was protecting herself from the world. I knew immediately she was a very fearful woman.

"I'm not happy that you're teaching children about altruism, Ms. Holmén," she said tersely.

I sat and took a slow breath, letting it out over my cup of tea. I had offered to make her a cup, but she refused, pushing the cup to the side. She wiped her hands on her slacks.

"Mrs. Reynolds, could you please share why Tommy shouldn't learn about altruism?"

She shifted one side of her backside on the small chair just as the Vice-Principal, Brandon Smith, stepped in and sat at the table. He nodded at me to let the conference continue.

At this point, I realized that Tommy's self-realization would not come to fruition, no matter what we had hoped for. Brandon held Tommy's file, indicating that his mother was taking Tommy out of my classroom and our school.

"He doesn't need to learn to share. Besides, he doesn't want to get germs from the other children."

"Ah, I see," I said. "One of the things the children learn about altruism is that what they give to the world can come back in incredible ways, even though they should never expect anything in return."

"My Tommy doesn't need that. He'll just be disappointed."

Brandon shared several stories from parents whose children were under my tutelage. She pursed her lips as if I were teaching the kids to banish the boogeyman from under their beds.

She then shared something very telling about her relationship with her husband and how she was projecting her disillusionment onto her son.

"Tommy is a very fearful boy. He wakes me up often in the middle of the night since he sleeps with me, and ..." she continued, but the words melded together.

My brain short-circuited at that point when she mentioned her sleeping arrangements with her almost nine-year-old son. Brandon raised a nearly imperceptible eyebrow and dropped his gaze. We both realized there was more going on than a stubborn child.

Tommy was the product of his upbringing. He had no sturdy soil to help him grow his roots and become an independent young man contributing to society. He left the school shortly after to become another teacher's concern. About three weeks into his time there, I received a call from his newest school. They came to the same conclusion: Tommy would always struggle until his mother learned a new way of parenting, or his father could spend more time with the boy, teaching him resilience and autonomy.

So many Tommys are the product of helicopter parenting, tiger mothers, or lawnmower parenting styles, which lead their children down a path and discourage independence and responsibility. These nicknames aren't very complimentary, but they all show a semblance of truth. When an adult feels a child could never learn to survive without micromanaging every aspect of their existence, they will never understand the skills to navigate this big world.

At this point, I reflect on Mother Nature. Every mammal mother knows that the formative years are when their younglings must learn to understand the world they are in or suffer and possibly die.

A video went viral on social media, showing a beautiful example of this parenting style. The video shows a wise mother mare walking her foal toward an electrical fence. You can see her withers flicker on her shoulders, displaying her discomfort of having her foal learn what this strange wire can do. The colt can feel its mother's uneasiness, nervously flicking its little tail. Trusting its mother, the foal walks closely next to it toward the fence. The mother urges her baby to go closer, then steps back. She waits patiently for her little one to touch the fence with its soft muzzle.

Suddenly, the foal's nose is shocked by the sharp snap of the electrical fence, and it kicks up its legs, running from the offense. The mother trots over to her young one, giving it a reassuring nuzzle, and they both walk away from the fence unharmed, but with a critical lesson the foal will never forget.

We, too, as parents, must guide our children into situations that may present them harm if not taught about the harmful object or situation in the first place. Think of the fireplace, the sharp corner of the coffee table, and the stovetop, to name a few. We don't want our children harmed, but never presenting challenging situations under loving guidance is also a great disservice.

We must sometimes make our children uncomfortable to show them the skills they need to survive independently. The old mare knew she would rather teach her foal than have her foal learn the hard way.

But what about the parents who inadvertently present their fears and distrust of the world to their children? These children then bear the burden of these stressors until it becomes a learned behavior. I saw it so often each year with various students.

Fear of germs, not wearing the right clothes or hairstyles, not being beautiful enough, fear of taking risks, not feeling worthy, and lacking self-confidence. So many children are taught that the parent is the ultimate authority. However, what if that parent has a skewed worldview, like Tommy's mother?

Remember, teachers only represent 30% of what a child learns directly! That is a small amount, considering they spend nine months with their students! That means a child learns through play, taking risks, and learning through failure. Sadly, many teachers feel that the child is doomed to fail if they don't tell the student how to think, when, and how often to think.

Many teachers also inadvertently teach that failure is wrong, so it's best not to do anything. It's up to the teacher to teach their students how to do it right. This brought me to tears one day in front of my fifth-grade class. I do not cry easily, so this even shocked me.

It was the second week of school, and we were in the middle of our morning routine, where I presented various problems in Math, Science, and grammar.

Some skills they were familiar with and were practicing, while others were new challenges, so I could see how much time they needed to spend on each new subject.

Two-thirds of this Fifth-grade class consisted of students I had taught prior in the Third grade. Many former parents requested me when they learned I was moving to Fifth grade that year.

I was determined to see how much my previous students had learned in Fourth grade and wanted to challenge them even further in their Fifth-grade year. So, when I began correcting the Morning Warm-Ups, I was utterly shocked when my old students told me that they were taught in Fourth Grade to leave a problem blank if they didn't know how to do it.

"Wait, what? You mean you were taught last year that if you were unsure how to do the problem, leave it blank? Then what?" I asked the class, walking around the room to see the blank answers.

Brandy answered promptly, "Teacher So and So told us she would just give us the answers if we didn't know how to do something."

I stopped and repeated her answer to ensure I heard it correctly. I took the iPad that controlled the whiteboard in the front of the room in my hand and closed it. I moved to the front of the classroom to sit on top of a free desk, propping my feet on its chair. I sat there in silence, which made my students squirm.

Chad knew what was coming. "Yes, Ms. Holmén. She always told us that if we didn't know something, she would tell us the answers."

"Did Miss So and So ask for different ways the problems could be solved?" hoping to redeem my colleague. The students with this teacher all shook their heads, 'No.'

My heart was breaking for the lost year of learning for my students. "What does that say about you, Chad?"

He looked around the room. I could see my more confident students realized this would be a reckoning of how teachers fail their students.

"Does it mean she doesn't believe we are smart enough to figure things out without her?" he said nervously.

I touched my nose, "Spot on Chad."

Silence. The students who didn't know me as well were squirming. My former students sat up to listen closely.

I couldn't believe the emotion that rose within me. I was the lioness, witnessing my cubs getting injured in a place where only good should come. With tears in my eyes, "Never, ever let an adult or teacher ever let you believe you aren't smart enough to figure something out, or at least give you a chance to try."

"Ms. Holmén, are those tears?" Chad and Brandy both spoke. Chad stood up and got me a tissue: sweet old Soul, Chad.

I took a deep breath and sorted my thoughts. Of course, I wanted the children to respect authority but not mindlessly follow someone who makes them feel less than.

"Thomas Edison said it best, *I have not failed. I've just found 10,000 ways that won't work.*"

Chad looked perplexed, "He said that?"

There was a commotion in the room regarding the quote and the inventor of electricity.

I nodded, realizing this was one of the most critical discussions I would ever have with my students to start the school year right. "You're going to find yourself in many situations every day where you might not have the answers, but you should at least put in the effort to try and test the waters. That's why you're at school, to learn how the world works around you. Sadly, not every teacher knows how to do that."

Where was the Serengeti when you needed it?

Chad and Brandy shared how Mrs. So and So never challenged them or just gave them the answers to questions they weren't sure of. Other students shared tales about teachers they had over the six years in school. Then the conversation migrated to how some of their parents never let them try things at home like cooking or mowing the lawn. It was ironic since they were talking about chores or menial labor that they would most likely want to get out of, but in essence, they wanted to be given a chance to try.

"So, think of the story I've been reading you, *Hatchet,* by Gary Paulsen. Brian found himself stranded in the Canadian wilderness after the plane he was in had crashed. Was there a teacher there to help save him? And what about Harry Potter? How is his story relevant to what I'm saying?"

The class spoke about how Harry was treated poorly by the Dursley family. If Harry hadn't tried new things and learned what he could accomplish, he never would have become a great wizard. Of course, it was fiction, but it struck home about effort and how failing brings you closer to success.

From that day in the classroom, all of my students were required to show an effort toward their learning. They were great at making each other accountable when working in pairs or teams. No one was allowed to get away with showing nothing.

Of course, I do not condone a Disney-fied world where parents and teachers are absent. I suggest we start challenging our children with everyday life skills to test how they handle situations independently. In my Gardener's Guide to Life, I'll cover some examples of things we can do with our children.

It also must be mentioned that the opposite of micromanaging parenting is the laissez-faire style, or the "I'm afraid to discipline my child" style. These parents are akin to the farmer who lets the weeds grow wild.

Without setting boundaries and rules, these parents teach their children that life will entitle them to anything they want. These children start life with a skewed perception that the world will bend to their every whim. Sadly, these children struggle from day one when the world shows them its unforgiving nature.

As a teacher, I need to guide these children to the electrical wire to see how the world can sting. I do this by consistently creating expectations that meet their efforts and only praising a child who puts forth an honest effort regardless of the initial outcome, just like the lioness teaching her cubs to hunt. If a cub runs off to play, he may miss out on the kill and not learn the necessary lessons to feed himself one day.

Consequences are essential for teaching children about the boundaries in life that should not be crossed. My students have faced several repercussions, such as poor grades, loss of friendships, detention, and loss of privileges, which have helped them understand the importance of respecting boundaries. Every consequence has a story behind it, and each story depicts a stubborn child learning to realize their true potential. As facilitators of their betterment, we are responsible for encouraging them to achieve their full potential.

***

Sometimes, a teacher needs to burn down their classroom to demonstrate the choices we make in our daily lives that could bring us harm.

Boulder, Colorado, was experiencing its summer fire season, and several homes had burned down, so this was a concern for most families living on the outskirts of town.

My students rented their desks and earned "money" from various jobs they had in class. Turning in homework on time, participating in discussions, and producing good products during Center time all earned them an income. Money was taken away by poor behavior and negligence toward work and assignments. This teaching style is called Classroom Economics, and it taught my students a lot about how the real world works.

We had just learned about home insurance since most of my class made enough money to 'buy' their desk and own it for the remainder of the year if they maintained a certain balance in their checking account. There was much discussion regarding how insurance worked, and many children who rented their desks didn't see the need to protect their rented homes. A few homeowners also decided not to buy insurance because it meant they couldn't afford to buy Game Day on Fridays.

Game Day was created by several students who asked one day about entrepreneurship. Chad and Brandy had already opened up small businesses. I allowed them to open their businesses on Fridays during Lunch hour for students who could afford to attend their businesses. This spurred many other students to open businesses on Game Day once they earned enough to purchase the business permits.

I realized we were in an economic boom in the classroom, and some reality of how the world works was necessary. So, I decided to "burn" several houses and rentals down to prepare them for those unexpected trials we all have in life.

The children lined up outside the classroom door one morning. I stood somberly outside their room. "Children, I am sorry to announce that the fires raging around our town have hit inside our classroom."

Those who were paying attention collectively gasped and screeched. I told the students to enter the classroom, stand in the back of the room, and not go near their "homes."

Inside the classroom, I had draped six desks with red bulletin board paper large enough to cover all sides of the desks. I had picked the names randomly. The students were not allowed to go into their desks to retrieve precious items or books.

The children moaned when they saw they fell victim to the 'fires.' I guided those homeless to a large kidney-shaped table in the back of the room. You would have thought a death occurred while the rest of the class guiltily got ready for their day.

The victims sat quietly at the table while the rest of the class meekly got their books, pencils, and checkbooks out of their desks. Those students could start their morning lessons, though their faces were guilt-ridden. There were several who gloated and teased, which gave me the idea to talk about humility, compassion, and empathy at a later time.

The children at the table had many questions, so I wrote them down on a tablet on the whiteboard. *How do we get our work done? Can I get my lunch money out of my desk? Did I lose all my books? Did I lose my money if my checkbook burnt up?* The questions were endless.

I didn't answer any of them to allow them time to think about their situation. I had the rest of the students finish their morning assignments while those without homes talked amongst themselves.

"All right, class, let's clear our desks. Please take your chairs and face our new homeless classmates."

Some of the children chuckled at the new term for their peers.

The barrage of questions came fast and furious. I let them answer them on their own with very little guidance.

Several students shared, "Now I understand how those families must feel losing their home, Ms. Holmén, and I just lost a desk."

I took this opportunity to teach a new word: "Does anyone know what it means when you can feel and understand someone else's pain?"

"Apathy?" Tina said.

"Close, Tina. You mean empathy."

I had the classroom Secretary write the word on our Classroom Economics Vocabulary board under Insurance Claims and Insurance Premiums.

We talked briefly about empathy and how the classroom now understood that term.

Then, one of my students, Paul, stood up. "I'd like to donate some of my money to our homeless, Ms. Holmén. I think that is called philanthropy, but I'm not sure."

Even though he was wealthy, Paul was not known to share with his peers, doing extra homework or projects to earn more money. He was socially awkward but well-liked.

"You are right, Paul. You would become a philanthropist by donating money to the homeless or needy."

The class decided to donate funds to Paul, who would divide the money for each homeless person. This excited the children to help other students who technically had nothing.

Finally, students began asking when they could return to their 'homes. 'Here is where our lessons on the purpose of insurance came into play. Weeks prior, I decided to teach the students about insurance and why their parents had a choice to carry it or not. This day was now their trial in the Serengeti. Who's home was protected, and whose was not?

Three of the six homes that burned down had home insurance so they could return home after lunch recess. The other students without home insurance had to stay at the table for the rest of the day.

I notified parents a week before the 'experiment' to encourage conversation and discussion during homework that night. The parents were excited to learn how it went, and I sent home a detailed letter about all their children learned that week.

The class was interested in how insurance worked and how it felt like gambling, whether you would ever need to use it or not. The students gained empathy toward their parents' plight in paying insurance premiums or going without insurance altogether.

I understand the importance of providing students with a safe and secure learning environment. That's why I always strive to find innovative ways to help students explore the natural world without putting them in danger and bring the world to them in a way that allows them to understand the risks without experiencing any pain or harm.

Like the wise mare, I guide them through the intricacies of the natural world, showing them the beauty and complexity of the environment while ensuring their safety and well-being. Whether through interactive simulations, virtual field trips, or engaging multimedia content, I am committed to providing students with an enriching and fulfilling learning experience that is fun and educational.

Zen Gardens

Zen gardens are intended for relaxation, meditation, and contemplation. Every plant, rock, and sand is given a special place in an effort to create harmony, tranquility, and balance. Nature is represented from a minimalistic point of view.

CHAPTER NINE

Opening minds, one sheep's brain at a time

BRINGING REAL-LIFE SKILLS INTO OUR CHILDREN'S LIVES

My twenty-five years in front of thousands of children have me concerned over our children's state of mental health in recent years. These are my boots-on-the-ground observations.

More and more children are being diagnosed with processing disorders, as well as behavioral disorders. These conditions can impact a child's ability to learn and interact with others during challenging school and social situations.

As awareness of these conditions grows, more resources and accommodations are needed to support children with processing and behavioral disorders. Parents, educators, and caregivers must work together to identify and address these issues early on so that children can receive the help they need to thrive.

My observations are entirely anecdotal. However, when you witness many distressing conditions developing in a vast number of our youth, you must, at some point, sit up and take notice.

I decided to approach this concern by teaching my students Mindfulness and the neuroscience of the mind. If there were a pinnacle moment in my teaching career, Mindfulness and brain-based studies would be my most profound lessons.

But it was more than that. I realized that society has lost touch with connecting with themselves- the metacognition part- thinking about how you *think*. How are your thoughts impacting you and the life you want to have?

It was my fifteenth year in the classroom, and I was contemplating leaving teaching. I was becoming numb to the fact that our education system did not create strong, resilient children. I wanted to create something more meaningful than memorizing multiplication tables and cursive writing. I wanted them to think deeper. That's when I discovered the neuroscience behind Mindfulness for children.

Goldie Hawn, the actress we know for her comedic stints in movies and television, is also a philanthropist. In 2007, through the efforts of the Hawn Foundation, she created a mindfulness program for children called MindUp. It contained fifteen lessons on teaching children how their brain works and how Mindfulness affects their brain chemistry and behavior.

I studied her program thoroughly and expanded it, creating a year-long program. I extended the lessons to make more meaningful connections. I also knew practice makes perfect, so creating a year-long program would ensure the lessons stick.

I began the first week of school that year with my third graders staring at a shiny, sticky sheep's brain placed on a newspaper in the middle of their group's desks. The sheep were donated from the local university's agricultural program.

Each student wore gloves, and a parent was there, ready to follow my instructions on peeling away the sections of brain matter with a scalpel. Three students chose not to attend the class that day, which seemed to be more about their parents' beliefs about eating meat than about doing science. Sadly, the three students stated later they wished they stayed in the classroom after hearing from their peers how awesome it was to see a real brain.

They learned that the prefrontal cortex is the executive decision-maker, helping us with emotional processing, memory, and self-reflection. The amygdala triggers our fight-or-flight response and the emotions of fear and anger. The last part of the brain that was taught was the hippocampus, the memory bank, where our memories are stored.

What surprised them the most about the brain was that it doesn't discern between good and bad thoughts and memories, false memories, and lies. It is just a filing cabinet that stores what we experience. A brain cannot filter out lies, so a person's brain can be filled with many misconceptions and false beliefs. Judgment and discernment come from our mental capacity, which was another lesson to be covered later in the year.

The following lessons were about how each child handles challenges. I started easy at first to help me learn which students needed more support due to trauma and behavioral issues. I called these students my 'red flag' students. They were easy to spot. They were the ones who could not embrace the lessons since each lesson meant vulnerability, and this perception of being exposed to the unknown was scary for them.

They stuck out like a sore thumb. "Please sit with your hands on your lap, palms facing upward." This task was simple enough to follow, but here was the clincher. "Please close your eyes and breathe out of your nose." For some reason, my students who had issues based on trust, authority, or family dysfunction would not close their eyes. It was as if they did; they would be at their most vulnerable with me, and truly trusting the adult was difficult at best. I tested this theory out for years, and the list of students was highly accurate.

By the end of the day, I had given the list to our counselors. Shockingly, each student already had a file on their behavior issues. However, some of them were not actively involved in any form of intervention counseling. MindUp was becoming the gold standard for identifying students with challenging behaviors.

Ask a classroom of third graders to stand up from their desks, and you'll see chairs fall over, desks scooted out loudly, and a general cacophony of chatter. I asked them to stand, and the chaos was precisely as mentioned, with a few students running to the door, thinking we were leaving the room. Oh, how I loved it when a lesson revealed itself so quickly! I then asked them to sit back down. The same racket ensued as they plopped themselves down in their seats.

I presented my students with a challenge: "I'm going to ask you to do a task. But first, we are going to learn about Mindfulness. Mindfulness is doing a task without any thoughts or judgment—just doing the task at hand."

I asked them to raise their hands above their heads and pat the tops of their heads slowly without making a sound. I then walked them through what they might have thought about while raising their hands and patting their heads.

"Some of you might have resisted raising your hands right away or raised your hands but then stopped when asked to pat your heads. Maybe that was because you were embarrassed to do that. Some of you did it without thinking and just did it. Some of you might have thought, 'well, this is a strange request,' and others weren't listening in the first place, eventually mimicking what everyone else was doing." The last observation elicited a laugh out of the guilty offenders.

"When you do something mindfully, you do it without judgment. The task is done completely without putting negative or positive thoughts toward it. You will complete the task calmly and precisely, as best you can, without judgment."

I shared that my least favorite chore at home was doing the dishes. I felt it was a daunting task, and I could mostly talk myself out of doing them until the dirty dishes took over the sink and countertop, to my chagrin. However, one day, I decided not to let the little voice in my head talk me out of doing the dishes. I decided to do the dishes without thinking about anything else.

I concentrated on the temperature of the water and counted the pumps of liquid dish soap. I focused on the lemony scent. I picked up a plate, washed it thoroughly, and placed it on the drying rack. Not a single thought went into how I felt or other things on my mind, just about doing the chore in front of me.

Each thought went into the act of washing dishes. Pick up, wipe off, clean and scrub, wipe and rinse, then dry and put away. No other thoughts entered my mind. By the time I finished the chore, I felt rested and relaxed. I also felt accomplished and satisfied with a job well done instead of rushed or not done at all.

I asked the children to think of something they did not enjoy but had to do. Some talked about picking up their dog's poop, doing homework, having to play with a younger sibling, or cleaning up their bedroom. They all moaned, thinking about the offensive chore.

"Let's practice doing something mindfully until you get it. When I tell you to, you will *mindfully* stand from your seat and push your chair in. Then you will stand there facing me. This means you will stand up, move around your chair, and push it in properly without showing any emotions except doing the task at hand. Any questions?"

They showed me they were ready, and I commanded, "Please *mindfully* stand and push in your chair."

You could hear a pin drop. Each child moved meticulously without a sound. Their faces showed their delight at how different it was to move as a mindful collective.

Brandy asked, "Ms. Holmén, I saw some of us smiling while we did it so well. Was that judgment, too?"

"Yes, it is, Brandy. You see, you had to have a thought that made you smile. Just as you have a thought that makes you upset or angry, even smiling at the thought of doing something well is judgment. Of course, if it makes you happy, you will likely do it again the same way."

The class took to the challenge and wanted to perform more mindfulness tasks. I created more complicated tasks each day until they did most actions mindfully.

By the end of the week, Chad challenged the classroom to walk into the cafeteria mindfully and then eat mindfully for the twenty minutes of lunchtime. I was on lunch duty that week, so he thought it would be easy for me to monitor how they did with the great challenge: clever, old Soul, Chad.

I stood up on stage where the duty teachers stood to monitor the large room of students during lunchtime. My class filed in without a sound and moved deftly through the room to their seats. Some moved to retrieve their hot lunches, while the cold lunchers sat and opened their lunches without a sound. The other students and teachers immediately noticed the difference between my students and the rest of the room.

My colleague, Janet, walked up the steps to me and motioned me to silence the microphone I was holding.

"Have they been acting up today?" she whispered, motioning to their table.

I laughed, "They've been learning about mindfulness all week, and they challenged themselves to eat mindfully today."

Janet watched my class from her vantage point. She noticed everyone was eating everything in front of them, and nothing was going to waste. She also noticed that the children seemed to have a trickle-down effect. The younger students, the following table over, were watching their older classmates eating in such a systematic way. Without any provocation, the entire room was silently eating. She was blown away.

Suddenly, our new principal came out of the office door into the cafeteria. She began screaming at the room, "So, are you all in trouble with Ms. Holmén today? I should take away your recesses for the rest of the week!"

Janet stifled a laugh, "I'll let you deal with that," she whispered, stepping down the stairs. I turned on the microphone.

"Hello, Mrs. *New Principal*, "I spoke quietly into the microphone, watching her put her hands on her hips, ready to scold the whole room.

I continued, "The children are learning about mindfully eating. Aren't they doing an amazing job? The teachers and I have noticed that barely any food is going to waste!" I motioned around the room. "My class decided to challenge themselves today to see if they could mindfully eat without judgment in a full cafeteria, and I can see other children know how to eat mindfully, too."

Students from other classes suddenly sat up straight and began to eat quietly. I took advantage of the impromptu lesson and taught the whole room to eat mindfully. Mrs. New Principal just stood there.

I noticed we had a few minutes to practice, so I had each table mindfully throw away their trash and line up against the wall. Mrs. New Principal almost seemed peeved that the room was doing precisely what I asked. Egos are hard to shed, I thought.

The ladies who cooked the meals were so delighted that one of them approached me on stage and took the microphone to praise the almost two hundred and ninety students for how amazing they were.

Mrs. New Principal left the room without comment.

With the cafeteria eating mindfully, cleaning up, and throwing away their trash mindfully, I let them know they earned themselves extra time to play outside. It was a natural consequence since little time was wasted doing things mindfully. They cheered silently and excitedly as they left for the playground.

The lunch ladies asked if we could do mindful eating with them for the remainder of the week. I obliged and worked with them on the positive reinforcements needed to keep it going. I walked into the office and was not surprised Mrs. New Principal wanted to talk to me.

"You can't just go and implement a new behavior policy without passing it by me first," she exclaimed.

I could see the school nurse and secretary roll their eyes at their new micromanaging boss, neglecting that this 'technique' created a positive environment for the children, teachers, and cafeteria workers. And it was my student's idea in the first place. What's the saying? Pride goeth before the fall.

"My students wanted to challenge themselves with their neuroscience studies. They asked if they could mindfully eat today, and sorry to say, it spread throughout the whole room. The ladies have asked that I try it for the remainder of the week."

She looked at me as if I had asked the students to have a food fight.

I realized that adults were their worst enemies when finding solutions to problems. Asking children for an answer can lead to innovative thinking compared to a closed-minded adult set in their ways. I asked the children to see the weeds and find a positive way to eliminate them without destroying the growing flowers. Mrs. New

Principal wanted to stomp on the weeds, killing them and the beautiful flowers growing amongst them.

My students thrived that year, and so did those who came after for the next ten years I remained in the classroom. I found a way to motivate them in all aspects of their learning by making them mindful of their choices and behaviors beginning on the first day of school.

Mindfulness made an even bigger impression on one of my students when his mother entered my classroom one day after school. She was crying, and I was nervous this could be another Tommy situation.

In kindergarten, her son Jake was labeled with Oppositional Defiance Disorder or ODD. In plain English, it meant he was impulsive and quick to anger. He was one of my former third graders and now attended my fifth-grade class. Jake was small for his size, but he carried a big bark and sometimes a fist toward those that upset him.

We were into the second week of school, and mindfulness activities were in full swing. I taught them breathing techniques to calm their amygdala so they could access their prefrontal cortex to help them learn or manage themselves after something stressful or exciting occurred.

Jake seemed to flourish. He was making friends, seemed genuinely interested in learning, and became a happier child. I didn't attribute this to anything I had done at the time. I thought he was growing up.

Brandon, the vice principal, shocked the class on this fateful day. Without knocking, he opened the classroom door with a grand flourish and pretended to admonish me for not seeing Jake in the office much that year. Brandy and Chad knew immediately that Brandon was teasing.

"I'm very disappointed in you, Jake. I haven't seen you in eight weeks, or has it been longer?" He put his hands on his hips, challenging Jake.

Jake, at first, was embarrassed. I could see his face redden as if he had committed an offense against another student on the playground. But then his face softened, realizing Mr. Brandon was teasing him.

"Um, I think it's been at least three months, Mr. Brandon," he said, his eyes beaming. "Do you miss me or something?"

Mr. Brandon walked up to him, shook Jake's hand, and then handed Jake a special award for students making incredible progress in their behavior and academics. It's a spontaneous award for those who need that little bit of extra recognition and reinforcement that what they do is making a difference.

The class stood up and gave Jake a round of applause. He blushed terribly but allowed the love to wash over him. Chad leaned over to me and said, "We've all seen a big difference in Jake. He's a different person now."

Jake's mother surprised me after school that day, entering my classroom and sitting at my table. She was wiping tears away. "Ms. Holmén, I can't thank you enough for these mindfulness lessons you teach the children. I've seen such a huge change in Jake. He's now doing it at home several times a day. He's even asked for a meditation area in the house where he can go and calm his amygdala."

My eyes couldn't help but shed a tear or two with her. Jake entered the room with a beautiful bouquet in a large French ceramic vase, the silk sunflowers towering over him. The bounty of learning was summed up in a beautiful bouquet of silk flowers I would keep in a special spot in my home. My garden was blooming.

"Ms. Holmén, can I show my mom the Zen Master job I get to do in class?"

Jake turned off the classroom lights and took out a little battery-operated votive candle. He explained that after lunch, the class gets out their votive candles if they choose or find a spot in the classroom to meditate and calm their amygdala with their breathing. He also took out a paper labyrinth for the children who preferred an active form of meditation, like tracing the lines in a maze. Both techniques, he explained, will calm the brain for learning.

He turned on my whiteboard at the front of the room. He brought up a slide show he had created with quotes of wisdom from everyone, including Aristotle, Thich Nhat Hanh, Gandhi, Lincoln, Michael Jordan, and other exemplary people. The little Zen Master then turned on instrumental music, rounding out the environment and fitting the mood.

His mother opened up her arms with tears streaming down her face. Jake walked up to her to take in the embrace. Incidentally, the family was still reeling from the divorce, and Mom and Dad were not getting along. The years between the third and fifth were wracked, with Jake getting suspended for several days for hitting another child with a chair.

I saw the calmness in both mother and son that year. I had watched this family grow and nurture each other into a cohesive unit.

She shared, "Jake now teaches his father to take the brain breaks you taught, and take a step back and calm himself before engaging in something."

I could only pray that Jake would take these skills and keep them close to his heart for the years to come.

***

The last six years of my teaching career allowed me to teach Mindfulness to over fifteen schools and thousands of students. The school district had just adopted the MindUp curriculum I had been teaching in my classroom, so it was an easy transition for most teachers to have me introduce those lessons to their students.

During this time, I realized that many teachers were nervous about teaching these new skills to their students. It was odd since it was such a powerful tool. The realization occurred when I led eighth-grade teachers on what to expect from their students when they did something mindfully.

"But what if my students don't do what I asked?" one teacher asked nervously.

The question shocked me, but it was warranted. I knew many teachers feared their students' retaliation, but it was mostly because they hadn't worked on building a rapport with their students in the first place.

In my years of teaching, I realized that we don't train teachers to build rapport or establish trust with their students. We hand over our children to adults who received a certificate from a theory-based curriculum taught at the university. I witnessed this first-hand after training hundreds of teachers how to challenge their students through the Gifted and Talented program I was assigned to as a trainer in enrichment.

Of the hundreds of teachers I trained, I only met a handful of teachers who were naturally gifted at teaching children. The rest were adults who knew how to follow directions, open a teacher's manual, and spew what was between the pages.

This is not meant to knock my colleagues. This warning is intended to help parents realize that we must select better adults who profoundly impact their children in the nine months they have to skew their child's perception of the world.

This is like preparing the soil of education for our children. How can we expect our children to flourish if ill-prepared teachers taint the soil?

I do realize, though, that the education system, as a whole, is broken. I have my thoughts on how to fix it. However, the most important thing a parent can do is pay attention to what is happening in their children's classrooms. Become the stewards of their learning. Ask questions and listen to your children's experiences when they are out of your care.

I want to share a few items to help your child find Mindfulness and resilience in their daily lives. Below are some websites and printables I used in my classroom to help students reset from stress or excitement.

I created a website on Amazon for my student's parents, which my students use especially near birthdays or holidays for gift giving—cleaver cubs, they are! The website contains information about my teaching approaches and philosophy and a list of books and tools I have personally recommended to parents over the years. This list has grown over the years as students' and families' situations change and parents ask for guidance. Here is the QR link to the website I shared with them.

During my twenty-five years of experience as an educator, I came across some incredible tools that helped families connect with their children in a meaningful way. By using science-based learning tools, I was able to help my students understand the immense potential of their brains. Interestingly, my exploration into brain-based studies also led me on a personal journey of healing for both my mind and body.

Labyrinths are an effective and practical tool that can be particularly beneficial for students who find it challenging to practice mindfulness breathing or meditation to calm their minds.

For many individuals, sitting still and clearing their thoughts can be challenging, and they may need a more active form of meditation to rebalance their thinking patterns. By walking through a labyrinth, a winding and intricate path leading to the center, students can engage in a physical and mental activity that helps them focus and relax. Traversing the labyrinth can be a meditative and calming experience that allows individuals to center themselves and find peace in the present moment.

There has been a renewed interest in the use of labyrinths in secular society in recent times. As a result, various institutions, including hospitals, have started incorporating them on their campuses to provide their staff and patients with a therapeutic activity that connects the mind and body.

For instance, the renowned Kaiser Permanente Hospital in Antioch, California, has installed a labyrinth to offer a healing experience to patients and staff alike. The maze has been designed as a pathway for individuals to take time out of their busy schedules to meditate, reflect, and relax. The hospital believes the labyrinth can help individuals reduce stress and anxiety, improve mental health, and enhance overall well-being.

There are three stages to the journey through the labyrinth:

Release: Begin by standing at the entrance on the edge of the labyrinth. Take some deep breaths. Gently follow the path at a pace that feels comfortable for you. Clear your mind and let go of all thoughts and cares.

Refresh: When you reach the center, you may want to stand quietly for a few moments. Visualize yourself in a peaceful place, breathe, reflect, and relax.

Return: When you feel the time is right, follow the path back out from the center. As you return to the world, bring the feelings or insights you experienced with you.

Many of my students loved learning about the labyrinth and asked to have one to keep inside their desks. I created a print-out of the famous Chartres Cathedral pattern they could use whenever they needed to reset. Many students loved taking out the labyrinth before a test or after a rambunctious recess. They'd trace the pattern with their finger, breathing slowly.

On one occasion, after a snowfall, I tromped through the snow to create a walking labyrinth. I took my students out early and walked it before recess; the class loved it. Several children, on their own, became stewards and placed themselves as guardians when the rest of the school was out for recess to teach the other children how to use it. I was surprised by the end of the day; only the grass paths showed through, and the labyrinth survived until it melted.

The labyrinth at Chartres Cathedral is considered one of the world's most significant labyrinths due to its historical, artistic, and spiritual significance. It was constructed in the early 13th century and is the most extensive medieval labyrinth still in existence. The labyrinth has 11 concentric circles and comprises approximately 261 paving stones, with a diameter of 12.9 meters. The labyrinth was believed to be used for spiritual purposes, such as pilgrimage, meditation, and penance. The design of the Chartres Cathedral labyrinth is unique in that it is based on a complex geometric pattern that is thought to have symbolic meaning related to Christian theology. The labyrinth has also been the subject of much speculation and interpretation over the years, with some suggesting that it may contain hidden messages or codes. Regardless of its true meaning, the Chartres Cathedral labyrinth remains an essential and fascinating example of medieval art and spirituality.

I also found physical labyrinths that you can hold in your hand, which is especially fun for my students. There are many ways to make a hand-held labyrinth, or you can purchase them online. Several families of students I taught purchased reusable labyrinths made of wood or metal for their children as gifts.

Here is the printable for you to share with your children or try them yourself!

Here is a link to a wooden hand labyrinth.

Life cycle,

In biology, it is the series of changes that the members of a species undergo as they pass from the beginning of a given developmental stage to the inception of that same developmental stage in a subsequent generation.

CHAPTER TEN

The impermanence of flowers

THE BITTERSWEET BEAUTY OF LETTING GO

Our children are like flowers. They are packaged from a bit of seed that grows inside our nurturing body and germinates into our lives. Their innocence and precious yearning bring years of color and joy. Then, the day comes in every parent's life when they must relinquish their children to the world, and our days may become a little less bright.

There is a beauty to this process—the process of letting go. Not only did I have to send my precious daughter into the world without my guidance and protection, much like the Lioness, but I also had to trust that she would take the lessons her father and I taught her to heart.

I also watched many former students grow into incredible adults, forging their way into the great unknown and leaving footprints of their accomplishments. Their parents showed reluctant pride and triumph that their children governed their lives with fortitude and hope, yet their days together were numbered.

However, I have also noticed the students who weren't quite allowed to spread their wings over the years. These young adults were taught to stay close to the nest and not wander too far. Though many parents desire to keep their fledglings safe and protected, they aren't allowing their children to test the waters of adulthood to see what they have gleaned over the years from their parents.

I believe in a nuclear family and all the benefits a family can bring to a young adult's life. But when a parent relies on that young adult child for their emotional well-being or confuses their role as a parent and best friend, the child is brought up with mixed emotions and confusion about the role of the *parent*.

As a parent, I learned early on that my daughter was only a visitor. I was to be her guardian, protector, and emotional support, but there would come a time when she was no longer mine. It was a profound moment I'll never forget.

McKenzie was two years old, playing on the floor of her room with some toys while I was in the kitchen preparing her lunch. I peeked into her room and watched her play, something many parents do on many occasions. They are just too cute to resist watching!

McKenzie put up her little arm and waved her little hand. "Mummy, it's okay. I can play by myself now. You can go."

My jaw dropped. I think I blinked several times at my little daughter's words, realizing I was only shepherding my little girl until she would be on her own. She was not mine to keep for my enjoyment.

From that day on, I knew I had a role - a role I enjoyed immensely, but there would come a day when I had to let my little girl fly. It was a keen awareness that she was her entity, a separate Soul here to explore and experience the world.

There is no denying that there was a tug on my heartstrings. I wanted our relationship to always thrive, but I would have to get used to the fact that it may be from thousands of miles away.

I'm unsure if other parents have experienced this, but I realized I had such an important job to fulfill and only a handful of years to do it.

I also felt I had received the handbook of *What Not To Do To Screw Up Your Kids*- so to speak- based on my dysfunctional upbringing. My parents taught me much about what *not* to do, and I was determined to create a new legacy.

We had a very close mother/daughter relationship, always sharing each other's thoughts and dreams. However, I always knew McKenzie would eventually leave and that it would be to her detriment if I tried to thwart those desires selfishly.

Like the Lioness on the Serengeti, I had to let my cub go to explore her world. This was a challenging feat. I felt the tug at my heart when she was no longer in my vicinity, and I could see her physically and make sure she was okay.

Most parents want their children to be happy and well-adjusted. It's a one-way perspective since children expect their parents to "always be there for them" but not necessarily a part of their daily existence. It is a death of sorts. A parent remembers astutely their importance in raising this precious being to one day realize they are no longer needed except for emergencies. Children are happy to fly from the nest and explore their new world.

Learning our roles as parents comes from our past experiences as children. Some of us were brought up in loving homes with parents who naturally could share their knowledge of the world. Other parents were not brought up in such balanced households. This is where a family legacy of dysfunctional parenting begins and can lead to many generations of children growing into adults who perpetuate the same problems.

I knew my family was unhealthy, so how could I discern that what I was to teach McKenzie was different from what I was exposed to? I taught her through hands-on experiences.

I knew she and I might eventually move to another town, and finally, she'd be on her own. How would my little girl navigate such a large world?

When she was seven, I would take her downtown to ride the buses so she could learn to read the schedule and determine which stops to make.

We would stand on the curb as McKenzie chose where she wanted to go that day. The museum and then a cafe afterward seemed like a good plan. I stood back and watched her seek out the bus with the correct number on its placard. She'd take my hand to walk up its steps. She'd ask how much the fare was, and she deposited the change into the receptacle. I would stand there and let her take the lead.

McKenzie's pride in her capabilities made my heart sing. We rode the bus several times that month until I felt she wouldn't have to fear the unexpected delay or accidental mistake of getting on the wrong bus. Every risk teaches a lesson, and I was there to help her through it.

I expanded our travels to San Francisco, Chicago, and Los Angeles. Each trip brought more lessons, and it was fun watching my little girl grow.

This helped McKenzie in so many ways. She could now see the world as a place to explore and learn from. Eventually, after she graduated from high school early, she decided to visit Thailand to help a group of scientists reintegrate the work elephants from the local villages back into the wild.

She earned the income to cover most of the program's costs, and a day before her eighteenth birthday, she was on a plane to Hong Kong and then to Chiang Mai, Thailand. I remember her phone call at the airport, waiting for the last plane to take her to her final destination, a remote village five hours from the city.

"Mum!" as she called me, "I just saw a group of monks in their orange robes!"

I could hear her excitement of seeing things she had only read on the pages of her books.

We talked about her flight and eagerness to get to Chiang Mai, where she would stay at a hostel with other students her age attending the program. Then, they would take a five-hour drive into the mountains to a tiny village on the border of Thailand and Myanmar.

McKenzie spent three months in Thailand, experiencing the world, which was truly awe-inspiring. My little cub, who spent eighteen years under my tutelage, was now on her own path.

Now, this didn't mean my job was over. McKenzie had learned a lot, attending a four-year university in Boston and graduating with honors.

I witnessed from afar my daughter testing the electrical fences that were part of her growing up. It wasn't easy at times. I saw how the world she was experiencing shaped her views, and I worried that these encounters negatively influenced her perceptions.

I saw her at her weakest moments, wanting to wrap her in my embrace, remove all her pain, and keep her in my safe home forever. This is where I had to step back as a mother and realize McKenzie was on her journey of discovery.

Regardless of the soil I provided her and the lessons I taught her on how to fertilize her mind and soul, McKenzie now has her garden to create, and I am currently an observer of how it flourishes or not.

McKenzie had come to me over the years when she experienced something she needed some advice on or wanted to vent on how things didn't always pan out the way she had planned. I witnessed her trials and tribulations yet knew there was only so much I could do as a parent, giving my child autonomy. This was her time to learn how to till her soil, plant seeds, and see what blooms in her garden.

This is by no means easy as a parent. Early on, I realized I was McKenzie's litmus test. Just as every gardener must check to see if the soil is too acidic, every child knows their choices and actions are noted by their parents - if the parent is astute to their child's choices.

If McKenzie made a decision she was unsure of or was out of the norm of who she was, she would either lash out at me or disappear into her world, so I was not privy to see how her choices were panning out for her. Parents are their children's litmus test, whether the child likes it or not.

It wasn't easy during these times with her. I knew she sought my approval but had to learn to navigate with her compass. What child doesn't want their parent's approval? It was a natural yin and yang of testing the waters. She was on the proving ground for her choices.

Of course, there were times I saw where she was heading with a choice she was making. I could have told her, 'Absolutely not,' but where would that have gotten us? She wouldn't have learned by doing if I had done that. I would ask her if she wanted my advice. Sometimes, she consented; sometimes, she didn't.

There is a point when parents have to let their children make their own choices and mistakes so they can learn from them. I've had to let McKenzie go into the world she created for herself and told her I would always be there for her—a complicated stage most parents face.

However, there is an opposing perception that some children develop into adulthood: the absolute denial of anything the parent believes in. This is akin to a new gardener not taking the advice of a seasoned gardener. There are fundamental steps a person must take to make their plot of land flourish: taking ownership of their choices, responsibility, admitting when they are wrong, not blaming others, and the list goes on. When an adult child blames the world for their downfall or feels their parents failed them, victimhood is a natural stance that can occur. This stance is like a pestilence that overtakes the fertile soil, leaving behind disease engulfing the landscape.

This does not mean parents are right and adult children are wrong. This only means we, as parents, know the alkalinity of our children's choices. Our experiences – before we even had children – taught us the wisdom needed to discern the choices they are now making.

> Confucius said it best, "By three methods we may learn wisdom: First, by reflection, which is noblest; Second, by imitation, which is easiest; and third by experience, which is the bitterest.

From that meeting with Father Timothy many years ago, I learned that parents can advise their children, but ultimately, children must learn through their devices. If it brings them back into the safe folds of the family, then so be it. If they go off on their own to discover what else their experiences bring them, there are lessons in that, too.

Just as the Lioness must relinquish her wisened eye upon her cubs, so must we let our children go and interact with the world.

Surprisingly, there is something I have witnessed over my twenty-five years working with children, and it is the *survivor child*.

These children always take me aback when I meet them. They are their autonomous entity, capable of seeing past their family's flaws, discerning they do not have to become what surrounds them. These children come from homes with a true disconnect between the reality of the norms of raising children and dysfunction. I've witnessed homes with duct-taped windows, no heat, or dinners at the family table. I've even had students living in a refrigerator box with their siblings. It's not the classic home a child should be raised in.

Bryan was only eight years old when he entered my classroom. He was a sweet boy with a charming personality and well-liked by his peers. Although he seemed pretty worldly in his conversations with my teaching partner, he was respectful and courteous to everyone he encountered. By 'worldly,' I mean he understood the complexities of the adult world. His mother was a phone sex operator, giving up her job at a brothel when Bryan was born.

Although he didn't have a father figure, he seemed to have the self-confidence and intelligence to realize this wasn't the norm in society. He applied himself in all areas of school and knew the art of conversation and diplomacy, playing well with all sorts of peers.

Bryan, for some reason, had it figured out. He talked about his mom like an old soul talking about a distant relative. He spoke of her hardships and the men that came and went through their lives, though he never went into too much detail as to embarrass himself or the listener. He knew she was doing the job she was doing to support him.

He spoke of how he cooked for her and kept the home clean. Bryan always attended to his homework and came to school dressed and ready for the day.

I never met his mother. She did not attend parent-teacher conferences nor came to any school events. I had hoped to meet the woman who raised such a capable son, but that would never happen. Bryan finished elementary school and moved into the world, ready to make it his own.

What did Bryan have within him to understand his life didn't need to go in the direction that typically occurs with children from homes with trauma?

Our world perspective is shaped by our experiences and what we have learned. When we venture into nature, we can observe a natural balance and harmony among all living things. Every organism understands its role in the universe and how it interacts with the environment around it.

As a writer, I have always been fascinated by the power of perception. It is incredible to observe how individuals interpret the world based on their unique lenses. We all have preconceived notions, biases, and experiences that shape how we perceive people and situations. These perceptions, whether accurate or not, can create a person's entire world.

I vividly remember a particular incident that highlighted the impact of perceptions. I was invited to attend the juried competition for a Fellowship Scholarship for writers. As I sat in the audience facing the judges, I couldn't help but overhear snippets of conversations from several readers of the selected novels. My novel, *Churchill's Raven,* was amongst the semi-finalists. Some praised my work, admiring the vivid scenes and passionate narration. It warmed my heart to hear their kind words, validating the countless hours spent honing my craft.

However, not everyone had such positive opinions. A young woman spoke of not appreciating anything having to do with war. She preferred the poetry that was being juried against my manuscript. Her face twisted with disdain, and I could almost feel the negative energy emanating from her as she tossed my synopsis to the chair. It was disheartening to witness such a sharp contrast in perceptions, especially considering the effort I had poured into my creations.

This incident made me realize just how subjective perception truly is. It dawned on me that no matter how skilled I am as an artist, I cannot control how others perceive my work. Each person brings their own biases, preferences, and personal experiences, making my art reflect their perception.

Perceptions hold sway not only in the realm of art. They shape our interactions with others, influencing our relationships and how we navigate the world. Biases based on race, gender, or social status can result in unfair judgments and prejudice. These misconceptions can hinder personal growth and prevent us from truly understanding and empathizing with those around us.

Understanding the power of perception has taught me to approach the world with empathy and an open mind. It encourages me to question my biases and seek a broader understanding of diverse perspectives. After all, perception is never set in stone, and it is through dialogue and genuine curiosity we can bridge the gaps created by differing perceptions.

Ultimately, it is crucial to remember that right or wrong perceptions shape our reality. By recognizing this, we can work towards creating a world that embraces diversity, fosters empathy, and allows for personal growth.

Bryan's perception of his situation was not that of a victim but that of someone who knew he had to create the world he wanted and not rely on adults to provide it. He cultivated the soil that made up his life and planted seeds of hope and dreams.

Of course, there are so many scenarios that affect children's development. They come in all shapes, sizes, personalities, and characteristics, just like our Earth's millions of plants and animals. With this variety, a child succeeds and fails in numerous ways, but the perception of the world is crucial.

When I saw the post on Facebook, I was beyond shocked. This family was the ideal family. I knew the parents and all of their children. I had spent time with them on field trips and watched them at local sporting events and get-togethers.

The parents were both professionals but were also devoted to their children. They had excellent communication skills and a healthy marriage. They were the couple that often went on date nights and couple retreats to rejuvenate.

The children were all top students and engaged in many activities they requested to be a part of. So I was blown away when I learned their middle son had taken his life.

The whole community on FaceBook was reeling with the news: so many questions and no real answers. Our hearts broke for the parents and siblings' loss. Was it an accident? Was there an underlying illness or mental health issue no one was aware of?

The parents went into seclusion for several years, and their other children went through the paces of school and eventually continued their lives, though much heaviness seemed to surround them.

A few years later, I met up with a family friend. I inquired about how they were doing, and my friend shared the family's conclusion about the loss of their son.

"It seemed to be his perspective on the world. Nothing more than that. We all saw personally the love and devotion they gave to each other, so nothing else could make sense of it."

She described the mother and father attending counseling to understand their son's actions. Even the counselor said there was nothing the parents could have done to change the scenario. When someone's perception of the world is so skewed, there is nothing anyone can do except to support and guide that person to their realization of reality. Until then, that person will keep perpetuating their false beliefs.

The parents did not see any indication of their son's misconstrued thoughts, except he was the more thoughtful child and more sensitive to the world around him. They felt he was more of an observer than his older brother, who was more active and engaging. They appreciated the differences in their children and helped each one pursue their passions. So, when this travesty occurred, it was like being hit by a tsunami on a beautiful summer beach. It rocked their world so unexpectedly.

It's instinctual to want to change someone when we see them heading toward their destruction. However, we can all think of a time when someone told us what to do, and we didn't take their advice, only to learn later they were right.

Why is that? Why do we knowingly think we've got it all figured out?

Put yourself on the Serengeti, and the answer becomes more apparent. Although the Lioness taught her cubs survival skills, it's up to the cubs to utilize her teachings. We must learn to trudge through our path in this wilderness called life, learn from our mistakes, and hopefully make better decisions next time.

This family recently welcomed a new baby and is working through their grief together. Their adult children are all impacting our community by becoming active members of mental health organizations and taking on professions to help others. Despite this tragedy, they are forging a new garden with plants to nurture and help bloom.

Annual, Biennial, and Perennial plants- Annual plants complete their life cycle in one growing season. Biennial plants are planted in one year, grow through the year, grow on, and flower during the following year. Perennial plants grow strong year after year.

CHAPTER ELEVEN

The Friends Garden:

CULTIVATING QUALITY BONDS IN THE GARDEN OF LIFE

What would our lives look like if we didn't have friends? It would be barren and lifeless, that's for sure. Friends are the wildflowers that grow over vast landscapes, coloring our days with liveliness and nuances. But why are they in our lives in the first place? Why are friends a part of our growth equation?

Collectively, friends are considered the family we wanted but never had. Of course, this sounds all rosey and idyllic. There is the saying: a friend for a reason, a season, or life.

We meet people from all walks of life in a myriad of ways. They may appear due to a job association, or they may be our neighbors. You might have met in a parenting group or become fast friends in a yoga class.

No matter how you meet, they enter your life to teach you life lessons. The lessons could be for them to learn or for you, but you will learn a lot about yourself through the friends you keep and the complex world of human nature.

I've had numerous friends over the years, though there was a period in my life where I found quality friends far and few in between. I would call them more acquaintances since friendships must be nurtured like newly planted seedlings, allowing roots to grow long and deep.

When I say quality, I mean the relationship should be on equal footing and respect. The caliber of friends reflects the level of growth you want to maintain in your life. Perennial plants last for years versus annuals that don't have the fortitude to grow over time. Annual friendships may have been enjoyable at the moment, but they also revealed their purpose. You may have clung together during a time of insecurity or unsureness, but it was never meant to last a lifetime.

Friends of high caliber are like perennial plants that bloom year after year. Perennial plants can last for years, producing flowers and foliage, and have deep roots that help them withstand storms and droughts. High-caliber friends have a solid foundation of shared experiences, values, and emotional bonds, enabling you to overcome life's ups and downs. They are dependable, supportive, and can always be counted on to be there for one another through thick and thin.

So, what is the key to having these confidantes in our life?

They are akin to the timely quote from First Lady Eleanor Roosevelt. "Great minds discuss ideas; average minds discuss events; small minds discuss people." I found many people fall into the category of talking about people. It is human nature to inquire about mutual friends, family, and acquaintances, but one should be wary when it's done out of mean intent, jealousy, and scorn.

I have found this to be the best litmus test for quality female friendships. When a group of women get together, where does the conversation go? Is it idle gossip? Do they speak about others to share that person's downfalls? Is there banter consistently antagonistic?

Or are they genuinely concerned with action statements like, "We should get Alexa out of the house more," or "I think I should make more of an effort not to be so negative with Wendy."

It is important to remember that whatever people talk about in your presence will likely be about you once you leave.

Men don't have the same motivation when talking about other men. They share facts. The most significant difference is that it only goes so far. No grapevine of gossip ensues.

According to a study called *The Truth About Gender Differences and How We Speak,* researchers found that men and women have different communication styles. The study found that men were likelier to engage in "instrumental" conversations, which focused on facts and problem-solving. At the same time, women were more likely to engage in "expressive" conversations, which involved sharing emotions and personal experiences.

Another study, *Gossip, and Gender Differences: A Content Analysis Approach,* explored the idea that women are more likely to engage in gossip than men. The study found that women gossip more than men and that gossip was more common among women's friendships than men's. This supports the idea that men are less motivated to gossip when talking about others.

Many of us need that confidante to vent to when hurt or angered. I vent to get my emotions off my chest to better deal with the situation without letting heightened emotions get in the way of the message. For me, it is always about the message, so a confidante can help edit our words and feelings to see things more clearly.

However, you cannot do this with any person. I have made this mistake with several women I thought were of this rare caliber to hold the message close to the heart and be my sounding board.

Having someone take your words and share them during a time of heightened emotions and vulnerability is like having your crops stolen just before harvest season. All the hard work you've put in to nurture and grow your friendship is suddenly taken away from you by the betrayal of another person, leaving you with nothing to show for your efforts.

Sadly, I was very trusting and carefully gauged how I treated and respected friendships and assumed they would do the same. Their thoughts and worries were safely put in my *vault of trust*, never to be opened without their permission. Women who betray me don't realize what a trusted friend I am. Shame on them!

No one is an island, though. We need one another to share our concerns, worries, joys, and sorrows to truly understand life. Having a confidante to trust and rely on is invaluable. Quality friendships are essential for emotional health and well-being. Building strong relationships takes time and effort. It requires both parties to invest deeply in the relationship and practice mutual respect, honesty, trustworthiness, loyalty, forgiveness, understanding, empathy, and friendship.

When your words are used against you, the betrayal says more about the betrayer than anything else. It suggests that the willingness to use someone's words against them reflects negatively on the betrayer's integrity, empathy, and moral compass. It indicates a lack of respect for the other person's feelings and a willingness to manipulate and hurt them for personal gain or satisfaction.

It also raises questions about the betrayer's intentions. Are they seeking to inflict harm out of malice, or do their unresolved emotional issues drive them? Understanding the underlying motivations behind using someone's words against them can provide insight into the betrayer's mindset and emotional state.

Was it jealousy or inferiority to make them feel better about themselves? This list is not exhaustive when one betrays another's confidence. When it does happen, it's time to weed out our choices and move on. Second chances can occur, but you could introduce an invasive plant that could take over your garden once graced with love and trust.

Betraying someone's trust by sharing confidential conversations can be complex, especially when it involves women. Different psychological factors and individual differences can play a role in this behavior. Not all women engage in this behavior, and the reasons behind it can differ from person to person. However, some common explanations can help us understand this phenomenon and may help us recognize the betrayer better.

Insecurity and jealousy can contribute to such behavior. Women who feel threatened by a close relationship between two other women may betray their trust to gain power or control over the situation. This behavior can stem from deep-seated insecurities or a fear of being excluded or replaced.

The desire for social validation can also play a role. Some individuals seek attention and approval from others, and betraying someone's trust can be a way to gain recognition or acceptance within a social group. They may believe that sharing confidential information enhances their social standing or reinforces their sense of belonging.

Lack of empathy is another factor contributing to betrayal. Individuals who lack empathy may not fully grasp the impact of their actions on others. They may prioritize their needs or desires over trust and confidentiality, leading them to betray someone's confidence without fully considering the consequences.

Competition among women can also contribute to betrayal. In some cases, individuals may view relationships with others as a competition for resources, attention, or status. This competitive mindset can lead to a willingness to undermine others by revealing private information or secrets.

The social dynamics of gossip and the spread of rumors can also influence a woman's decision to betray another woman's confidential conversations. Gossip can serve various functions, such as bonding within social groups, establishing hierarchies, or gaining information about others. Some individuals may engage in gossip as a means of achieving social currency or as a way to feel included in social circles.

It's important to note that these explanations are not exhaustive, and individual motivations for betraying trust can vary greatly. Additionally, it's crucial to avoid generalizations or stereotypes, as not all women engage in this behavior, and men can also betray confidence.

We all wish for organic friendships, with both parties having an equal interest in keeping the budding relationship alive. Over the years, I have learned that a quality friend beats out quantity any day. Nurture and hold on to these women, for they are few and far between.

I wasn't able to grow many childhood friendships. It's not that I didn't have friends; I had many. However, from age 8 to 18, I went to work every day after school, leaving no time to nurture those burgeoning friendships.

It's not like I didn't try. I have a fond memory of a friend who lived just a neighborhood away from me. I'll call her Racoon Girl since she was tending to a new batch of orphaned raccoon babies and invited me to help her feed them.

Raccoon Girl was a beautiful tom-boy, active in sports, and had many boys chasing her. She was friends with almost everyone in our elementary school and well-liked by our teachers. When she invited me to her house after school one day, I couldn't resist. We took the bus, and instead of staying on until my stop, I jumped off on hers, reassuring the bus driver our mothers had already planned it.

We fed the babies until their tummies were warm and fat, putting them in their nesting crate to sleep their milk comas away. She took me exploring behind her house in the creek, searching for salamanders. We played with her Barbies and played Marco Polo in her pool until our hands were wrinkled and water-logged. Her laugh was contagious, and we got along so well—Ying and yang of sorts. Having a girl as a friend was new since I was so used to being with my brother and his friends.

The day is seared into my memory because it was the first and last time I really recall being able to play with a friend during the school year. Work came first, and summer was when we could escape to play with the kids in the neighborhood, but those memories were short and fleeting.

I didn't have any issues meeting people and maintaining casual relations. They were the friends I'd sit beside in art class or orchestra, and I'd meet them at football games or the roller rink.

They'd whisper to me who they liked or tell me about the latest gossip. I never shared their confidence since it was all too much to remember.

The best friends I did make ended up moving away at the end of the school year, so the process of finding one started all over again. Rake, weed, plant, nurture.

I had friends in each cliché clique. The groups were of all sorts, like the Jocks, the Cheerleaders, the Math Club, Biking Team, and the Goth and Stoners, though I had a more challenging time relating to the latter two. I was never left behind if we were in groups for a team event. So, in a sense, I never felt out of place or without someone to connect with. That is saying something since those teen years can be brutal.

It was, however, strange that I could never connect with girlfriends like you see on TV or in books. The girls who had known each other since primary school and could list each other's boyfriends based on haircuts or the shades of eyeshadow of that decade never existed in my life. The girls who planned girls' weekends to a resort in Aspen to catch up on the gossip since their college days—the YaYa Sisterhood type. I was not lucky enough to have created such life companions. It's not like I didn't want them or couldn't grow these deep bonds. It was that I often moved after I left for college.

I moved away from my hometown at age eighteen and never came back. Yes, FaceBook was what we transients used to keep 'in touch,' but we would never have that daily connection no matter how many photos you took of the new puppy or decadent dessert that sat before you on vacation.

I became an observer of how friendship dynamics worked and how they were intertwined with expectations and social norms. Many people were willing to maintain friendships regardless of the quality of the relationship. Numbers were more important than character and quality.

I accepted that I wasn't to have many friends, but the quality of my friends counted. I'm still searching for like-minded people with the loyalty, trust, and fortitude necessary to grow deep roots that can last a lifetime. I've only found a few of my authentic True Blues—those that I could trust and rely on, and they would be there for me, and I would be there for them.

Lucy Barns was one of them. We met at work, teaching. I loved the way she taught her students—calm and exact yet loving at the same time. She also had a life outside of teaching, so her interests were vast. She was a single mother like me, and I admired her ability not to let things get to her. If they did, she was resolved to solve it—sooner or later—without drama and many affirmations.

Lucy and I connected over an effortless conversation one day between bathroom breaks. She stopped me in the hallway and asked if I was reading anything interesting. It caught me off guard, so I answered her without thinking twice about the book taking up my evenings.

"The Science of Mind by Ernest..." I began as she finished my sentence.

"Holmes?" she said incredulously. "You mean you're reading it in a group with a Practitioner?"

I smiled. I wasn't sure if Lucy was mocking my intelligence, which wasn't like her. "Well, no. I found it at a center I visited a few months ago and thought I'd like to read it. I'm almost done if you'd like it."

Her smile almost turned Cheshire-like, then bubbled into a kind laugh. "Do you know it can take some people years to read and understand Holmes," she said as the recess bell interrupted our conversation.

Lucy came by my classroom that afternoon and told me about becoming a Practitioner at the Center for Spiritual Living. This explained her almost Zen-like nature, which I admired when I first met her.

Lucy became like a mentor to me. I met with her privately like a patient would a counselor, but our friendship extended into dinners and chats during lunch breaks in each other's classroom. She was non-judgmental and always went deeper into conversations, wanting to know the person's intentions behind their actions. She spoke of how we were all connected, and each of us had a greater purpose. Lucy was integral in much of my growth during those years. Eleanor Roosevelt would have loved her!

Although she left our school and continued into the ministry, I still feel connected to her today, though we have let time and distance separate us.

Lucy is a treasured friend. She appeared to me during a time when I was allowed to reinvent myself. Newly divorced and feeling free for the first time in two decades, Lucy brought me solace, friendship, loyalty, and trust. I often think of her and miss her in other social circles. Quality women like this are hard to find.

That brings me to Leanne. I met her early on when I met my husband through a mutual friend. His smile grabbed me with his strong jaw and gray goatee, reminding me of the recent show I had been watching about Vikings. He had the same features as the benevolent and strong Viking King.

Leanne was close to the Viking King's family, which was a godsend for me. Dating a widower is no easy feat. I don't necessarily recommend it to anyone. You immediately have a target on you that you're not supposed to be in this person's life. I was keenly aware of this fact when meeting various groups of The Viking King's friends and family when we began dating.

The first two months of dating were blissfully heaven since we sequestered ourselves to tiny social gatherings amongst close friends who were helping the Viking King get out into the dating world. These memories of our honeymoon romance keep me going through the not-so-good times.

The honeymoon faded when we attended a trendy local event. It was when the reality of human emotions and perceptions can derail any happiness you might build at the beginning of a love affair.

We were at a local motorcycle fundraiser with thousands of riders from all over the region. It was our first major social event together as a couple, and the day couldn't have been more perfect. It was like watching the Viking King rise like a Phoenix from the ashes as he was greeted by old friends and colleagues congratulating him on dating after three years of grieving his beautiful life partner.

I received hundreds of hugs and kisses from people whose names I barely remember. Our faces hurt from smiling all day from everyone who came to wish us well. I met many of his adult children's friends, who gave us even more hugs and kisses. The Viking King was finally among the living, and they loved witnessing it.

Many spoke to me about what a wonderful man the Viking King was and how happy they were he found someone. My heart grew ten sizes that day. But, by the night's end, word got out that Dad was with a woman for the first time, and reality set in for both of us. Our life together was not necessarily an island to bask in our love. There were opinions and emotions about a widower dating at all. Widowhood had a different set of 'rules,' and we didn't have the book.

Although the Viking King promised me he wouldn't let the outside world affect us, I knew it was a promise he couldn't keep. The thoughts were too close to home. I was an outsider with no right to enter into his world. The space beside him was never to be filled. It was sacred, and I was defiling that space.

When I met his tight circle of friends, the men and most of the women greeted me happily and enthusiastically. They were sincerely happy to see their friend in the world again, breathing and finding life. However, one of the wives — whom I felt her leery glances—wondered who this 'replacement' was in their dear friend's life.

She met me with a strained smile. I was astutely aware I was not supposed to be there, and it would take time for this friend of the Viking KIng's to realize he was teaching her what life was about—seasons change, and we are not in control of any of it. Thanks to the Viking King's guidance, and the other wisened women helped her work through her grief in a healthy way.

He showed such divinity during our infancy. Through his grace of acceptance of his great loss, the Viking King saw he had no other choice. He knew he was loved once and was blessed to have been given another chance at love.

I became friends with a few of these women but knew I was still an extension of the Viking King. I listened to the stories of their beloved friend, whom they had lost, with a sincere desire to get to know the woman who shaped much of the Viking King's beliefs and perspectives. I learned of his marriage and his family. The stories reassured me he was a fantastic man.

Initially, I contacted these new friends to build a relationship with them. However, it became evident that they felt the Viking King provided all my needs and women folk weren't needed in my new life. I was never a part of their daily and weekly texts, calls, or female gatherings.

The Viking King would encourage me to call or text to stay connected, but it would only last that conversation, and inclusion into the group wouldn't occur. It wasn't organic. We weren't on equal playing grounds. They had their circle, and I was outside of it. I belonged to their friend, and he was happy.

Leanne, however, embraced me in her life, and we became very close, confiding in each other's daily lives. She gave me insight into the Viking King's perspectives and understood how tough it must be to be the new companion in an otherwise tricky situation. She was realistic in her worldview and knew he and I were well suited for each other.

Men have a hard time understanding the pecking order in women's groups. There are so many unspoken rules to follow that don't exist in men's circles, so it was hard for the Viking King to grasp what I was experiencing. I had also gone through this before, after my divorce, but for reasons I still will never understand.

My ex-husband, Jack, and I were married for almost 20 years and had our daughter, McKenzie. We had made many friends, primarily through work and his coaching. Our social calendar was packed with group dinners, camping trips, and happy hours that kept us busy most of the time.

I was grateful for the outside companionship, though it was strange. The women were the wives or girlfriends of Jack's friends. Although we went out as couples, I was never invited further into the group of women. It stopped at couple-events only.

I was never invited into the circle of women for monthly birthday dinners, ladies' nights, or girls' weekends. Even Jack couldn't figure it out.

Was it insecurity or jealousy? I hardly felt like a woman to envy with the hardships in my life. I often invited them into our home, but it was never reciprocated.

During my marriage, I finally reached out for help, as I could no longer endure Jack's physical and emotional abuse. This was the truest test of friendship for me, as I had counted at least a dozen women in our group of friends I saw often. But unfortunately, only one of them, Amy, stood by me through my trauma and divorce. It's been twenty years since then, and I've realized that no single woman except for Amy was there for me during that difficult time.

Was the stigma of divorce still alive and well in the 21st century?

It was a rude awakening, realizing how little fortitude these women had to protect one of their own.

Lucy and a few other rare women were my litmus test. I knew I needed to seek elsewhere for female companionship. I needed women with depth and breadth in their spirit. Loyalty and trust among women take a lot of discernment to find.

I was a woman who 'had it all together.' One of the Viking King's female friends once told me that. So, in a sense, I did not need female companionship because I had my ducks in a row. These were her thoughts. It made me laugh when this woman told me her perspective. It was after I had told her I was feeling very lonely—nothing the Viking King had done, but I needed other outlets and female companionship.

However, upon observing the behavior of the women in this group, I began to feel uncomfortable participating in their activities. As a petite person standing at just 5 foot 3 inches tall and weighing 130 pounds, I cannot drink half a bottle of wine on a nightly basis, nor do I want to try. Once the drinks started flowing, so did the ensuing behaviors. I let the Viking King know it would be best for me to stick to the monthly dinners with these friends and leave it at that. But there was something else I noted.

It was odd watching this group of women during my interactions with them. There was an enabling spirit among them. They fed each other the vines of negativity, mistruths, stories, and gossip, with no one questioning the others' motives, insecurities, or ill beliefs. When one of the women finally went on a health kick to lose weight, which meant she wanted to cut back on the drinking, she was met with the other women showing up at her house with bottles of wine!

Later, she confided in me that staying healthy with friends like that made it hard. She loved them but couldn't ask them to respect her boundaries. They needed a conspirator, and she feared the ramifications if she questioned their choices.

How sad she felt she had to sacrifice her health to keep her within the group! She succumbed, stating that the women needed an outlet for the trials and tribulations in their lives, so the drinking continued.

This group of women saddened me. Each had many unique gifts to share, but their internal struggles kept them from shining their talents into the world.

Oddly, each one suffered from various health conditions. They were feeding their bodies and minds with weeds of enablement, negativity, and denial, and this was reflected in their health.

When a second woman in the group decided to take her health into her own hands and made incredible strides in losing weight and making significant advances at the gym, she was met with temptations and snide remarks, like she had committed a great travesty in putting her 'ducks in a row.'

Eventually, she distanced herself from the group because she realized that her health and well-being were more important. She no longer wanted to enable harmful behavior. She confided in me often, and we decided it was best for us to only see the group on special occasions. We loved them and their wonderful qualities, but it was difficult to improve ourselves without their support.

Enabling someone's skewed perspective can be detrimental because it allows them to continue living in denial or ignorance. By constantly rescuing them, you prevent them from learning how to solve their problems or face the consequences of their actions. This can be especially damaging in the long run, leading to a sense of entitlement and a lack of resilience.

It's essential to support and encourage others, but it's equally important to help them develop the skills and confidence they need to navigate life's challenges independently. Doing so empowers them to become self-reliant, essential for personal growth and well-being. Imagine how this group of women could have grown if they had supported their new journeys to a healthier mind and body. Women empowering women is a powerful asset in the female collective.

When it comes to our relationships, whether they are platonic or not, we all have to make a conscious decision about how much time and effort we are willing to invest.

Reflecting on these relationships, I realized my gut instinct was correct. It was a valuable lesson to learn about the dangers of acting out of obligation, which are damaging effects to your mental health, such as guilt, limitations on personal growth and fulfillment, and the potential for manipulation and control.

Over the years, I've gained insights into the female experience and how women behave. Having a twin brother has given me a unique perspective on how men view the world, which allowed me to view things more objectively.

Sadly, women compete against other women. The reason is typically for the hierarchy in the group or a man's attention. It can also be competing with other women with their clothing, looks, or position.

Our most primal nature is to find a mate, and women still feel the need to compete for that position, and it can bring out the worst in the female collective.

Being a woman is no easy feat. Being a confident woman is even more challenging. I have no desire to compete with my fellow species. I believe in women's empowerment and strength and providing shelter when needed.

I've had so many conversations with the Viking King trying to explain the complexities of women. He still shakes his head. So, I try to show him through other genres.

Many movies demonstrate this point, with the female psyche as the central theme. The 2004 movie *Mean Girls* delves into the complexities of female relationships, shedding light on various aspects such as friendship, competition, jealousy, and the impact of societal expectations.

Directed by Mark Waters and written by Tina Fey, the film explores the dynamics among high school girls and their challenges in navigating their social hierarchy.

One of the lessons that *Mean Girls* teaches is the concept of female competition. The film portrays how girls often feel pressured to compete with one another for popularity, attention, and validation. This competition can lead to toxic behaviors such as backstabbing, betrayal, and sabotage.

The character of Cady Heron experiences how engaging in this competitive mindset can negatively impact her relationships with other girls. Through her journey, the movie highlights the benefits of supporting each other instead of tearing each other down.

Mean Girls also explores the issue of jealousy within female friendships. The film showcases how jealousy can arise when one friend perceives another as more attractive, successful, or popular. This jealousy can breed resentment and create a toxic environment within a group. The character of Janis Ian represents someone who harbors deep-seated jealousy towards Regina George due to past experiences. This aspect of the movie demonstrates how jealousy can erode trust and ultimately destroy friendships if not addressed.

Mean Girls also addresses the influence of societal expectations on female relationships. The film depicts how girls often conform to societal norms and expectations to fit in or gain acceptance. This conformity can lead to the withholding of individuality and the formation of supportive relationships.

Gretchen Wiener's character exemplifies this struggle as she constantly seeks validation from Regina George and conforms to her standards. The movie encourages viewers to challenge societal pressures and embrace their true selves, fostering more authentic and meaningful connections with others.

It's interesting how this movie provides valuable insights into the complexities of female relationships. It highlights the detrimental effects of gossip, the toxic nature of competition, the destructive power of jealousy, and the influence of societal expectations.

By exploring these themes, the film encourages viewers to reflect on their behaviors and strive for healthier, more supportive relationships with other women.

I have experienced many negative aspects of the female psyche and how they keep women from sharing their authentic selves. The women I want to experience are the ones who constantly strive for an optimal yet simplistic life—genuinely and sincerely—warts and all!

Leanne and Lucy represent a health bond among women. They are one of those rare women who aren't afraid to tell you the truth, even when it smarts. Their self-confidence, intelligence, and lack of desire for any drama in their life make them extraordinary women.

I want to work with empowering women who promote mental and emotional well-being. Women often face societal pressures and stereotypes that negatively impact their self-esteem and mental health. However, when women uplift one another and challenge these harmful narratives, they create a space where self-acceptance and self-love are celebrated.

Once you put the energy out into the world of what you desire, it will come to you in ways you've never expected. Currently, the Viking King and I moved to a new state in a new community. I put it into my mind that I would attract women who resonated with me, and Ms. Leaf is one of them. When we met, it was like meeting an old friend after years of being apart. Her energy is light, loving, intelligent, and so open to the world. She desires the best in humanity, and she is an amazing mentor. Ms. Leaf, I feel, is like the loving sister I never had. It is strange how life will reflect what you give to the world.

Life as a woman can be incredibly challenging. Our bodies can be unpredictable, and we are expected to navigate the world like everyone else. However, I don't believe that women should have to act like men, nor should men have to act like women. Put aside "man-splaining" and ask a man what he has to say about the dynamics of female friendship groups. Their perspectives can be eye-opening!

It's time for us as women to acknowledge and embrace our unique experiences and perspectives, which allow us to see the world through different lenses.

The wisdom of womanhood can be awe-inspiring!

By fostering positive relationships based on trust, respect, and encouragement, women can combat feelings of isolation and build a strong support network. This network provides emotional stability during difficult times and promotes overall well-being, similar to creating a garden where your flowers can grow. Leanne, Lucy, and Ms. Leaf are my Sun and water, nurturing me to be my best self.

Seed

A seed is a mature ovule that comprises an embryo or a miniature undeveloped plant and food reserves, all enclosed within a protective seed coat. Seeds are a way of reproduction for all flowering plants. When a seed is exposed to the proper conditions, it will germinate into a seedling through adequate sunshine, water, and oxygen.

CHAPTER TWELVE

The Perfect Seed

THE POTENTIALITY OF EVERY HUMAN BEING

There are no perfect humans, though many strive for perfection. Unfortunately, we are born predisposed to DNA that can trigger a genetic variant when we are under stress or trauma for an extended period of time. These little "triggers," I believe, determine our exit point. Yes, we will all become part of the compost heap at some point—if you haven't fathomed this, then we should talk.

Many of us will go throughout our lives never experiencing these deficits in our DNA, like cancer, an autoimmune disorder, or other genetic variants. However, I feel these come to fruition for two reasons, and please remember, these are my opinions.

The first reason is we must have a way to depart from this world, as we have yet to discover a way to stay here permanently. Some people believe this decision is made before we are born and may come with lessons for ourselves or those impacted by our departure. Ultimately, it all comes down to the life lessons we must all learn, and experiencing death is one of the biggest ones.

Our adept DNA might not be our ultimate demise, however. We leave this planet in many other ways, and each departure will have a story behind it. Whether it is from our own hands or an accident, death tells its own story.

The second reason we may depart is we aren't expressing our Soul's purpose, and our bodies will reflect this discord. Like a garden exposed to toxins, poor light, or a neglectful farmer, it will reflect the effort and love given to it.

How many Souls come here and don't live the life they are meant to live? They feel like they were born with a hole in their Soul, missing a crucial key that will allow them to live the life most desired. They search throughout their lives for someone to fill that hole, only to realize they still feel empty.

An example of this is a man I met a few years after my divorce. I'll call him the Director. We met at a community function where I was in charge of greeting new people who had moved into the condominium community where McKenzie and I lived.

His stature caught my attention, standing over six feet tall with a kind smile. He wore a tan suit coat that seemed rather large on him and baggie jeans, accentuating a portly gut. I could see the look he was going for, but it missed its mark by being ill-fitting.

The Director had just moved into the area to work for the Boulder Film Production Office. During our conversation, he spoke about adjusting to his new surroundings.

We spoke a lot that evening about film production in Boulder, and he was surprised I was working on a screenplay for my film company. We shared our backgrounds in writing, and he told me about several screenplays he wanted to work on. By the end of the evening, we had made plans to meet up and see what we could do to make our screenplays come to life.

He offered to drive me home since the evenings were getting cold. As I walked to his SUV, he rushed to the door, which I thought was thoughtful until I realized why. When he opened the door, I saw half a dozen crumpled Fast food bags covering the seat, and several fell onto the ground. His apologies pierced my ears as I threw a couple of hardened french fries into a nearby bush.

"No worries," I said, trying to calm his embarrassment. "I'm sure with just moving in, it's hard to make a good meal at home."

He was ashamed, "I can tell you must not eat like this since you're so fit. I'm so embarrassed this is your first impression of me."

I had to admit it didn't check off any points in his favor. "Maybe you aren't in a place in your life where first impressions are your priority."

He looked sideways at me, and I realized I may have spoken out of turn. I didn't say it to be curt. I was telling the truth, something I developed after my divorce when the obvious was obvious.

"No, you're right. Though I think I'm ready to start meeting people," he said with a smile.

□I could see my words tumbling around in his mind as he drove down the street. "You know, I'd like to show you some of the artwork I've been collecting. Would you like to see them?"

□"Now? It's getting a little late, don't you think?" I said, unsure if I wanted to do the proverbial - 'going to his place' scenario so soon after meeting him. I checked my gut senses, and it felt right. He seemed to be who he was.

□"It's only to look at the art I've collected since you said you love visiting museums. I figured you'd appreciate what I've found."

□I nodded in agreement, and he pulled down his row of condos.

□After my divorce, my time with men was very poignant. Each man I met was placed before me to teach me another lesson. I wondered what the lesson I was to learn with the Director, and I was game to learn more. My intuition was growing. I could sense a person's energy when they approached me. I also noticed I was more attuned to McKenzie's energy to her chagrin.

□I could feel her emotions when I thought about her while she was at her father's. Often, I would text her, asking how she was doing or saying that I was thinking of her. She would tell me later that my text came in at the exact time when she needed it.

□The sense would come through my stomach region. I could feel a twinge or flutter or burn. Eventually, it moved to my heart. Now, however, there is no physical sensation but a knowing.

□It took practice, asking people questions, or paying close attention to what they said or how they behaved. I even joined a FaceBook group for people wanting to practice which type of intuition they had. Everyone has this ability; it needs to be practiced like anything else.

□I had looked over the Director that night, feeling only platonic friendship. However, something also compelled me to get to know this man further. I felt a nudge from the ether propelling me toward him, but not for the reasons I had thought that night. I figured it was time for my screenplays and writing to take their place on the proverbial screen finally. Still, life lessons don't come so blatantly.

□He walked me up the stairs to his condo. It was cluttered with the rummaging of antique and garage sales. His furniture was eclectic, yet there wasn't any place to sit. He had piles of assorted books, magazines, and boxes of unique finds all over his condo, which he hoped to sell for a reasonable price at one of the local antique auctions.

The Director prattled on about the various finds, one of which I was impressed with. He had placed an elegant Eames lounge chair beside the large picture window, nothing cluttering its soft leather seat or ottoman. I sat in the luxurious chair, looking around his place, seeing a man trying to put his life together.

"I can see how much you love this chair," I said, touching its buttery soft leather.

He walked me through the rest of his condo, pointing out each piece of artwork. He had a keen eye for art, and his photography was striking. He was talented.

He walked me to his bedroom, wanting to show me some art propped against the wall. Half of his bed was covered with papers and more clutter.

Surprised at my boldness, I looked up at him, "You know, Director. You said you hoped this move to Boulder would bring someone new into your life. How are you allowing that person to enter your life with all this taking up room for them?"

He put his hands on his hips in a daze, staring at his bed. "Wow, you know you're right."

We moved back into his living room, and I sat in the inviting chair.

"So, how long have you been in Boulder?" I figured he had just moved in looking at the unpacked boxes.

"It's been almost four months now," he said, moving a pile of camera equipment off his sofa. After the divorce, staying in Atlanta was getting harder and harder. My ex was seeing some guy, and I couldn't stop watching him flaunt his big business in front of me."

The Director's voice was pained as he spoke. I could hear the agony of the divorce still resonating within him. It must have been recent, I thought. Also, he was more concerned about the man than his ex. I was getting an etch-a-sketch outline of what made the Director who he was. I could sense his lack of confidence as a man regarding his marriage.

"When did you get divorced?" I asked, walking over to the bookcase filled with books on film production, screenplays, and photography.

The Director stopped rearranging his clutter and stood up. "It's been ten years."

I tried not to gape. I was shocked to hear the pain in his voice was so raw, assuming it must have been recent with the way he spoke about it. I realized there were a lot of unresolved issues he hadn't worked out yet hearing such emotion from him.

He spoke of his marriage to his ex and how hard it was to work with her, knowing she didn't want him anymore. It was good to hear he was honest about his feelings, which made him more endearing.

He removed his cowboy boots, placed them next to the couch, and walked into the kitchen to offer me a drink.

We shared mutual experiences about divorce, and he told me he stayed with her for his daughter's sake. I shared that we had that much in common. I could tell by how he spoke about his daughter that he was an exceptional father.

"I like to think I had to endure what I did with Jack to get myself a daughter like McKenzie," I added, putting some cheese and meats on a plate.

"That's exactly how I feel," he said, moving the food onto the coffee table.

We talked for several hours about film and production. He then shared a screenplay he wanted to develop and asked me if I wanted to be involved.

The Director was very animated when he spoke of his time in the nineties when he was involved with a film that won an award. It was the last thing he accomplished in cinema, and I wondered if his lack of self-confidence caused him to achieve less.

He was a location specialist and photographer for the Film Office in Boulder. He asked me to help him find sites for an upcoming production. I knew of some particular locations he needed, so we set another date to meet.

The evening was pleasant, getting to know this man and his history.

My eyes began to close, and he realized he needed to get me home. The Director reached over to put on his cowboy boots, and what I saw was interesting enough to make me take notice.

Now, mind you, I had seen many men don their cowboy boots living in Boulder, and it never dawned on me that there was a manly way to do this and a not-so-manly way.

The Director moved from the couch, sat on the floor, and grabbed his boots. He lifted his leg, then pointed his toes and slid the boot on, reminding me of a ballet dancer putting on her toe shoes. I was taken aback by the effeminate way it was done—not manly at all. I only say this because it was so noticeable. I felt embarrassed judging him this way. I asked another question.

"What happened for you to know there was a problem so soon in your marriage? You said you knew the night of your honeymoon."

The Director raked his fingers through his hair, then shook it back into place, "She said she thought I must be gay!" his hands opened wide over his head.

I couldn't complete my following words. His mannerisms were too poignant. I had wondered if his ex saw this early on and was concerned about his orientation. I didn't feel he was Gay. His effeminate nature was curious, and I wanted to see if my assumptions were accurate. I had known several effeminate men over the years, and it took a particular type of woman to find them romantically compelling. However, they made incredible fathers.

Later that week, the Director invited me to work on his outlines for a feature film we felt I could add to the female character. I walked up the stairs, and to my surprise, his condo was utterly transformed!

"Director, it looks amazing!"

Everything was in its place, and all the packing boxes were gone.

"You were right, Debbie. I needed to start doing things to make my place more inviting for someone to enter into my life and have a place in it."

He showed me his living room and then his bedroom, all neat and tidied. He pulled open several drawers, showing me they were ready for a partner to join him.

"Wow, good for you! This was a feat for sure!"

He beamed with pride over his efforts, which looked amazing. His artwork and photography on his walls finally had their place to shine.

However, I did get an inkling he was doing this for me. I became more keenly aware of any advancements I didn't want from him. Time would tell me more about this enigma.

We spent the next several days in his condo, going over his notes on several screenplays and choosing one to work on. It was an exciting dynamic since I was already familiar with screenwriting. I worked on one for about six months in the evenings after work. I had even purchased my LLC, Cool Beans Films, right before meeting the Director, so some of my interest in him was partly due to wondering if we were meant to work together in my company. So far, it felt right. I liked his screenplay and thought we could partner well on it.

Things started to unfold in our relationship that I wasn't expecting. I felt more confident with my intuition with the Director, even sharing some feelings and sensations I got when we spoke.

One night in particular was unforgettable. The Director spoke of his father and how much he looked up to him. As he talked about this man, I suddenly felt a presence in the room. I told him what I saw. The Director leaned forward, intently listening to me.

"As you were talking about your dad, I felt the presence of a man standing over you."

The Director's eyes widened. I wondered if my woo-woo talk would scare him, but I didn't care at that point, which surprised me, so I went for it anyway.

"He's wearing a long black trench coat, and I see him wearing a white hat and holding a briefcase. Was he a pilot?"

The Director jumped up from the couch in shock. "Oh, my gosh, can you see him?" his eyes wide.

"I… I can sense him standing there more than see him." I had never done that before, so it was shocking that I was correct. I felt my time with Anthony was proving beneficial, and honing my intuition was becoming more accessible.

The Director's eyes filled with tears, and he sat on the floor with me by the coffee table. He grabbed a tissue and wiped it away. I told him more of what I sensed from this man.

"I feel he is apologizing to you about his behavior toward you."

This caused more tears. I moved the box of tissues toward him.

The Director then spoke at length about his relationship with his father. I felt he had always hoped for his dad's approval, but I'm sure his dad saw the Director's softer nature and worried about his son.

I didn't tell him about that part. How could I tell him his father wished he needed to be more manly? The Director was soft and kind, and it was his nature to be that way. However, it was apparent that this had caused him a lot of pain since society expects a man to act a certain way, and the Director was different.

My intuition had proved very important in our relationship as it progressed. I would pick up 'hits' of what the Director was thinking and being able to read him, especially when he was being untruthful. This would also bring us to a breaking point.

His birthday was approaching, and he had always wanted to go to the Flagstaff House, a Michelin-starred restaurant with incredible views on the outskirts of Boulder. He asked me to join him.

It was a beautiful drive up the canyon road that summer evening. He spoke of his desire to travel, and I told him of my desire to stay in Paris for a month and write to get to know the city.

As we pulled up to the restaurant, he parked the car and let it idle, turning to me. "I promise you this: when we make this film and get our first royalties, let's go to Paris and work together on our next screenplay."

It was a beautiful invitation based on hopes and dreams we both wanted to fulfill, and I smiled at his genuine excitement.

□"We will have to see what comes to fruition," I said.

□We had arrived early to take in the vistas overlooking the mountains and Boulder below. Ben brought his camera to take photos and even surprised me by taking some of me. This is when I knew he was a talented photographer.

□He walked us over to the patio with the restaurant behind me and the beautiful vistas in front of us. The Sun was in its golden hour, so the lighting was phenomenal, and I felt confident in my black fitted dress, perfect for the occasion.

□I watched a young family looking through binoculars, laughing at the children begging to be next, unaware he was taking photos of me. He walked up to me to show me what he had taken. I was astounded to see how beautiful I looked in the pictures; it was the first time I had seen myself that way. I asked him to send me the photo, which he did immediately.

□"I've never seen myself that way. These are so good," I told him, swiping through the pictures, slightly embarrassed about my loving the way I looked.

□"You're a good subject, Debbie. Easy to capture your spirit."

□I laughed as I usually do when given a compliment. We moved to our table near the large panoramic window, the view now of the city's twinkling lights below. Dinner was super, and our conversation returned to the dream of living overseas and writing together.

□I began to feel an inkling that the Director wanted to further our relationship. Still, I was determined to keep it strictly to business. I made the mistake of letting him know.

□"I love the idea of us becoming a great writing team, producing films that matter. But let me bask in that for now- the possibility of what we could be."

□I realized my words were being twisted into something more. He took my hand, and a tear formed in his eyes.

□"Debbie, I will show you what a great producer and Director I am. You don't have to worry about Paris. We will have Paris."

□I left it at that. I couldn't burst his excitement. And besides, it was okay to hope he could become the man he was meant to be. I'd be his cheerleader, but romance would be off the table.

□The following weeks were busy with me teaching during the day and meeting with the Director in the evenings. McKenzie would roll her eyes when he came over, his exuberant greetings engulfing her. She would tell me he seemed like a lost puppy, and, at times, his innocence was overwhelming.

He would tell McKenzie that time with her made him miss his daughter more. His daughter was attending Georgia State and would graduate at the end of the year. Although he couldn't wait to see her then, he dreaded being in the same space as his ex. I mentioned he should work on releasing some of the pain he had from his divorce.

"I can't believe you said that," he said, closing the lid on his laptop.

"I'm sorry. I didn't mean to offend you, but it seems like you're holding onto a lot of anger for something that happened over ten years ago." I continued writing the scene heading.

His hands flailed in the air, "It was traumatic what she put me through!" He stood up and paced the room.

I watched him rant for the next five minutes, not saying anything to provoke a further explanation as to why he was worthy of great love.

"Sometimes I don't think you're on my side, Debbie," he said as he flopped back down to the couch.

"Look, I didn't mean to hurt you by my words. I think you're doing so many amazing things to grow into this new chapter of your life. Don't you think you should let go of the past and heal? Remember, she's not here in Boulder, but you bring her here often."

He looked at me, and I could see my words softening his demeanor. I also decided to take a break from him for a bit that night. He had been taking up most of my evenings, and I missed my mother-daughter time with McKenzie.

We worked on the script for the remainder of the evening, keeping the conversation light. Luckily, we got to a scene that I was to write. I told him I had a busy week and would check in the following week.

The Director didn't take my absence too well. He called or texted me most days, which I didn't mind, but I realized he must feel lonely. He only knew McKenzie, me, and a few people at work. I felt terrible, so I promised I'd stop by after I took McKenzie to her father's.

That night was full of shocking moments. It had been 18 days since I last saw the Director, and he changed in more ways than expected. I walked up the stairs to his condo to see candles lit at the table and the Director standing in a buttoned-down white shirt and new jeans. But what was more shocking was that he had lost a noticeable amount of weight.

"Oh, my gosh, you look great!" I said, giving him a quick hug.

He patted his almost invisible stomach. "I took your advice and revamped my whole way of eating! No more fast food for me!"

He escorted me into the kitchen to look at his pantry and refrigerator.

"Wow, this is great to see. How do you feel though?"

He stretched his arms high and exclaimed, "I feel amazing! I also sleep through the night now, so that's a plus."

I moved over to the couch and saw light appetizers with two bottles of Trappist beer on the coffee table.

"Oh, my favorite beer. I haven't had Trappist since my time in England," I told him as he took the cap off for me. We tapped our bottles and enjoyed the crisp, malty taste.

"How about we watch one of my favorite movies?"

"And which one would that be?" I asked as I settled onto the floor, leaning against the couch.

He turned on the DVD player and settled onto the couch behind me. We watched *Paper Moon,* which took twice as long since he had to stop often to discuss directorial notes, dialogue, and scene setting. I enjoyed his expertise and hoped he could keep up his momentum with our film.

Another Trappist led to another movie. I don't remember it at this point since after my third Trappist beer, I was thoroughly enjoying the intoxication and began giggling through one of the scenes I don't recall.

The Director joined in the frivolity of seeing me drunk for the first time, which also shocked me. I rarely ever drank to the state of a buzz since my experience with my ex led to some frightening behavior from him when he was drunk. I never felt safe around Jack. He drank most nights, so I made sure I was sober to be able to handle any of the aftermaths of his behavior.

That night, however, I felt safe for the first time with alcohol involved. I could walk home if needed, and the Director was harmless.

In one fit of giggles, the Director reached around from the sofa and embraced me from behind. He kissed my neck, which was a sensitive spot for me. I turned to release his hold when he took my chin and kissed me. I let the kiss linger since I was feeling no pain, and my response was slowed down to a crawl with the alcohol spinning in my head.

He crawled off the couch and kissed me again. I let him. We lingered until I realized this wasn't where I wanted us to go. We were working partners, and this could complicate things. It's amazing how the brain still works, albeit slowly. I knew I didn't want this to go any further.

I slid out under his embrace and carefully stood, the room slightly spinning. "I don't think we should go there."

He sat back on the couch, his face showing disappointment. "I'm sorry, Debbie, it just seemed the right thing to do." His voice trailed off.

"It's okay. We've been spending a lot of time together, so these things can naturally happen."

He stood up and hugged me. It was sweet, which was where I wanted to keep things between us. A lovely friendship that kept our working conditions uncomplicated.

I walked home to my condo that night, grateful things didn't go further. If it had, however, I wouldn't have felt like I would lose myself in the relationship like I had in my marriage. I could have a physical relationship without making it a lifelong commitment. I thought of giving us a try, but it was up to me and not him. It felt good to be in control of what I wanted this time. I controlled my Fate and desires and was allowed to keep them contained to what I wanted.

The screenplay was moving along. The Director decided to connect with some family and friends who had the perfect location to shoot the film. He asked if I'd like to go with him to scout locations since I was on break and McKenzie would be with her father.

I flew into Indiana and met up with him at the airport. He had taken an earlier flight to do extra work for a friend's film production company.

I walked outside the airport, where he met me in his car. He gave me a big hug, and I climbed into the car. His affection was still transparent, though I had to remind him we were work partners.

"I understand, Debbie, but things may change when you see our movie on screen."

Of course, I hoped to see it come to fruition. Would it change my feelings for him? It could—maybe. But for now, I saw a man striving. Was he capable of great success? That was not for me to decide. This trip, however, would teach me a lesson I wasn't prepared for. It was more a lesson for the Director than it was for me.

We reached the farm where the movie would be filmed. It was a working cattle farm owned by the Hampton family. They were gracious, allowing us access to the barns and the full range of amenities.

□The Director and I drove the entire property length, making notes and taking photos of potential scene locations. He was in his element, excited to have me there watching him work.

□Then, with an inkling of worry, I realized he was doing all this for me. His only motivation was to prove he was the man for me. I learned from my marriage that the motivation to change must come from within, *not from anyone else.* It was doomed to fail if the motivation to change was to obtain something other than their self-growth.

□This became apparent when we were given our sleeping arrangements in a renovated cabin near the main house. We said our good nights after a delicious meal made by Mrs. Hampton and were escorted to our cabin.

□The Director took my bags and brought them upstairs to a loft area. Two beds were separated by a large bookcase that acted as a divider between the two beds. He set my things on the couch in a sitting area and put his stuff on the larger bed.

□I made small talk, reviewed the notes from the day, and sat down at a small table to annotate the script where potential scenes could occur.

□The Director sat down next to me and took my hand. "You can now see that we are meant to do this together. Today could not have gone any better."

□I slowly took my hand away, moving toward my things on the couch. "It was fun today. The Hamiltons are a great family, and their son Josh was so adorable, wanting to show me his hunting blind down by the river. They've done a great job with him. He's going to be a very capable young man."

□I noticed I was prattling on about things, trying to move the conversation away from us. I climbed onto my bed with the script and flipped through the pages, discussing the next day's plan.

□The Director walked over and took off his boots. I made sure I didn't watch him remove them this time. Unexpectedly, he bent down and crawled onto my bed toward me. I laughed as I sat up, suddenly realizing he had a look of intention I was not interested in.

□I rolled off the bed and over to the table, "Director, I don't think that is a good idea."

□He stopped in his tracks and sat up on the bed, crossing his legs. I had to ignore his position, looking too much like a young boy than a sixty-year-old man.

□"I told you that, although I consider you a wonderful friend, I don't want to move in this direction just yet We are working partners, so let's leave it at that right now."

He smacked his legs. "But you see me accomplishing what we need to become a great team."

I wondered why this had to be an argument. He leaned back on his hands, looking up at the ceiling. I closed my notes and watched him for a moment. He pushed himself off the bed and stood by the table.

"This really shouldn't be an issue. Let's keep this professional and get the movie made."

His eyes welled up with tears. I moved from the table to create some distance. It occurred to me then why his ex-wife had enough. He was needy and did not understand his responsibility in the matter. This little tantrum was enough for any woman to want to leave.

"This movie will go nowhere without me. You realize that Debbie?" he said, sitting at the table with his head in his hands.

I blinked at his assumption. I knew I could accomplish anything I put my mind to, so his idle threat made no moment to me. I busied myself by unpacking my things. I couldn't look at him. This sixty-year-old man was falling apart if I didn't satisfy his purpose in his life.

"Let's finish our location shots, get some scenes written, and see where this goes- with production. We have so much to do to get this green-lit. I also don't need this taking up so much of my time. I have a job and plenty of projects to keep me busy, so don't go on about me needing you to get this done."

"Why can't we be more than just a writing team? There are plenty of writing teams that have both?"

"Tell me this," I asked. "Do you want to have this screenplay made into a film?"

"Well, yes, of course I do."

"Then that should be our only goal, nothing else. Prove to yourself you want this accomplished; take us off the table for now and concentrate on that, please."

I could have said more, but I felt my emotions beginning to boil.

He slinked to the other bed, lights out without another word.

We finished the shots and left each other at the airport, each going in our own direction for several weeks. He visited his daughter at college, and I flew home for a nice reprieve from the drama.

□While the Director was gone, I pulled out several manuscripts I had written throughout the years to see if any had that would make a great film. It was fun playing around with the scenes and fine-tuning the characters.

□Ultimately, I felt all films should be books first since a book could provide much more depth than a 120-page script. I decided that if things went wrong, I'd start working on my books again.□

□We worked on the script twice on the phone, but for the most part, it was quiet between us. I was grateful for the reprieve. The Director's energy was too much, too needy, like a toy needing its child to make it real.

□Luckily, I was busy at work, and the holidays were getting McKenzie and me out of the condo for her choir and orchestra practice.

□"So, how are things with the Director, Mum?" McKenzie asked as we drove through our favorite neighborhood decked out with Christmas lights.

□"Oh, he's being the Director, honey. I can't get over how he believes we must be a couple to work together." I felt it was important to share how men could misconceive things.

□"He hasn't tried anything, Mum, has he?"

□I laughed at her protectiveness toward me. It was sweet of her to be worried.

□"Why do men do that? Think that we have to do their bidding. He is such a wimp," she said, mimicking his hands waving above her head.

□"Now, honey, I understand what you're saying, but he's also a broken man. I see it more each time I'm with him, and it's not up to me to fix him. He has to want it for himself."

□Ironically, McKenzie was dealing with a male friend who was having the same issue. She spoke about how she and I seemed to have mirrored lives when it came to men once she was old enough to date. We compared notes and laughed at the similarities. I wondered if there was some cosmic reasoning.

□Did I need to experience these men first to teach my daughter the ropes? Maybe this was breaking the legacy my mother had started so many years ago.

□I was grateful, however, that McKenzie hadn't dated anyone - yet - like her father. To know the emotional and physical turmoil I had endured for so long would have had me worry endlessly about her.

□Luckily, she broke it off with a young man who was extremely needy. He was similar to the Director and felt McKenzie was the answer to all his heartache. McKenzie was kind to him initially, but toward the end of their time together, she had to become more blunt with his neediness. They ended it barely speaking.

The weeks without the Director taking up my time were light and airy. McKenzie and I enjoyed our Christmas traditions of decorating, baking, and seeing the lights. I had heard from him twice, and from those conversations, I realized he was not a sound man. My intuition kicked in full gear and did not disappoint me.

He called me one evening upset. "Debbie, I need to see you."

"What is it?" I could hear his voice breaking.

"It's my friend, George. He was killed in a car accident."

"Here? In Boulder?"

"No, he's in Atlanta."

I let him speak, but something was off. So, I allowed him to continue as I opened my laptop. I knew enough about fatalities to know they would be reported in the news wires. McKenzie saw the concern on my face and moved next to me at the table. I put it on speaker so I could type.

"Oh, that's awful. What was his name?" I typed as he spoke. "And, where did this take place?"

I scoured the local newspapers and even the local incidence reports from their highway patrol. He said it happened several days prior, so I knew it would be listed. Then, I checked the obituaries. Nothing.

"I see. Well, I am so sorry this happened."

"Can you come over? I need to see you right now."

I paused, looking at my daughter's face. She shook her head slowly. I took her hand and nodded reassurance.

"You know, it's late, and I need to help McKenzie with a few things before tomorrow. I'll stop by after work."

We hung up, and I walked McKenzie to the bedroom. "Wow, I can't believe it, Mum, he's that desperate to see you. How did you know he was lying?"

"I don't know. I just felt it, I guess."

I kissed McKenzie goodnight and returned to my laptop to confirm my intuition was correct. I wasn't sure if I would tell him that I knew. I would see if he would fess up or not.

Several days later, a second call confirmed I needed to sever my ties with the Director until he found professional help.

"Debbie, I need your help. My car was just hit while it was parked, and I don't know what to do."

"Are you alright?" I asked, turning off the stove to avoid burning my dinner.

He spoke about how he parked it on the side of the street, and someone side-swiped it, taking off the mirror.

"I have a great mechanic that could put on a new one."

"It's also the money. With that movie being canceled in Boulder, I'm not seeing that bonus this month."

"If your car got hit by someone else, you can get your insurance to cover it. Where exactly did this happen?"

He explained how he was parked right next to the ballpark entrance to take photos of a new art installation.

"That area has tons of cameras," I explained. "When you reported it to the police, they would send someone to check the cameras."

"I didn't report it."

"Why not? Insurance would cover it, and you said you needed the money."

"I was already in a wreck earlier this year, so I don't want my insurance company to know."

I felt like I was talking to a teenager whose prefrontal cortex was not fully developed.

"Okay, well, it sounds like you need to fix it so you don't get a violation."

He talked about work slowing down and how the film commission might rebrand itself. He was worried about his job.

"Maybe I could stop by your place and see you for a little bit?" he pleaded. "I need a friend right now."

I let him know I already had plans that night with McKenzie, and we left it at that. I could hear his glumness as he hung up. I knew our days were numbered, and I would have to let him know we were done with the screenplay.

Although the thought of letting go of the screenplay annoyed me, I felt exhilarated knowing I was finally making choices regarding the people I would allow in my life. He had become the proverbial weed, and my garden had no room for it.

Two weeks passed, and the Director invited me out for my birthday. He made reservations for the Flagstaff House. I was hesitant at first. I knew that if he made any moves toward discussing us as a couple, I would end our working relationship immediately.

The night was beautiful, with a fresh coat of snow on the pine trees, making everything so soft and perfect for the time of year. He pulled up to the valet and let me out. I walked into the restaurant and was escorted to the bar to wait for our table. The bar looked beautiful, with fresh-cut juniper boughs draped over and throughout the restaurant. A piano player played Christmas jazz to round out the merriment.

The Director met me at the bar, and we ordered some drinks. He seemed happier than I had seen him in weeks.

"I think I can acquire a Red Dragon to shoot the film. I have a connection with a local production company, and we can rent it from them."

I was glad to hear him talking business again. It had been a long time since we spoke like business partners. "That is exciting. Once the script is finished, we can approach talent, right?"

We discussed the necessary steps before we acquired permits to shoot. We also discussed the storyline a little more, and I mentioned that changing the female lead's motivation was essential.

"I want to make her stronger. She went through an abusive marriage, as we spoke about. I don't think her old high school sweetheart sweeping in to save the day is what our viewers want. Women want to see a woman taking the necessary steps to take control of her life- on her own two feet. If they become romantically involved again, it should be on her terms."

The hostess interrupted our thoughts as she escorted us to our table. It sat before the great window as a light snow began to fall. It was truly picturesque, and my mood was light.

"So, wait, you don't want Jenny together with Ben at the end?"

I took my purse and placed it on the empty chair beside us. "I want to leave that to the audience to decide. We don't need to smack them in the face with it. Ben is patient, giving her time to reconnect with the woman she has become. It shouldn't always be assumed the woman has to have a man in her life to achieve great things."

He squirmed in his chair uncomfortably as the waiter shared the specials and we ordered our meals.

☐"But this movie is about us, Debbie. I want it about our journey. You left an abusive marriage, and I want it to be our turn."

☐"Wait, what? So this movie is about our relationship? Is that what this is about?"

☐"Well, yes. Our penultimate will come together once it's on the big screen. I want the title to be *If She Needs Me*."

☐My mind went blank. It took every ounce of my being not to have a visceral reaction to his words. I couldn't believe we were at this crossroads again.

☐"Director," I paused, working the words around my brain. "I feel like it is all or nothing with you. I either give in to your pressure, or there is no screenplay."

☐He sat back abruptly, his chair scraping the floor. It caused other diners near us to take notice. The waiter served bread and our appetizers, causing a moment of breath between us.

☐I said in a lowered tone. "This can't keep happening. You can't seem to separate us and this project." I dug into my salad and pushed the miniature crab cakes toward him.

☐I took a moment and looked around the room, watching everyone seemingly having a good time. You could see the "first dates" with their broad smiles and hesitant hands. An older couple sat, hands touching, eating their meal in silence. Oh, to have an ease with each other would be wonderful, I thought.

☐I looked over at him, realizing he wasn't eating. He was staring at his plate with tears in his eyes. I was done at this point. I had never met a man willing to deface himself publicly over a disagreement.

☐I leaned over, quietly putting my silverware down. "Director, this has to stop. I can no longer let this continue if this is your behavior each time we disagree."

☐He stood up quickly, scuffing the chair again. "You know you'll never get a screenwriting gig unless you have me. You need a man to show you the ropes. Without me, you'll never go anywhere." His arms flailed above his head, and his voice cracked. I felt he was speaking to his ex-wife. He was no longer with me but was having a worrisome argument with her in his mind.

☐My heart tightened, wondering how far he would let this rant go. I noticed the man to my right sit up and place his napkin down. I motioned to him that things were alright, but apparently, more diners were taking notice.

☐I whispered, "If this is how it will be, Director, then I don't want any part in making this film with you. I don't think you have it in you to do this without it becoming an issue if we date or not. This is a worthy film, but we must give it wings first and see if it will fly."

He sat down, his mouth gaped, snot pouring out of his nose. I couldn't look at him.

"Not without you, it won't, and not without me. We have our Director and producer. So, you're just going to quit, Debbie?"

"Cool Beans Films is done with this project, Director. We had what it takes to make this a great film, but it's not about us as a couple. I thought you had the fortitude and desire to create something you've wanted for years. Now, it's just about if I sleep with you or not. No, Director. We needed to work first, then see if this was something to pursue. But for now, I'm not impressed. We're done."

I knew my words stung, but he didn't understand how absurd the conversation was AND that it was in public view. He had no semblance of etiquette, and I knew I had to leave.

The waiter arrived with our plates in hand. I stood up and grabbed my purse," Could you make mine to-go? I'll pay at the desk."

The Director was now in a full-on cry, taking his napkin and mopping his nose. I was utterly shocked at this man's weakened state and felt he was truly disturbed. I could see the diners near our table wanting to make space by turning their chairs away from this spectacle.

I walked to the coat check and then paid for my meal as the waiter handed me my container of food.

"I'm so sorry, Miss. That didn't seem to go so well." He leaned closer. "I think you're making the right choice, though. Do you need a cab?"

I nodded, then looked back at the Director, still sitting at the table. He sat like a wilted flower, struggling to grow and bloom without the proper nutrients and care, constantly searching for something or someone to fill the gaps in his perceived imperfect garden.

His sorrowful eyes drooped with a hint of desperation as if constantly searching for something or someone to fill the void in his life. His now unkempt appearance and slouched posture gave off an aura of defeat and desperation.

Standing at the entrance waiting for my cab, I observed the Director sitting there dejected, staring at his plate. He was in search of someone to complete his garden, I thought. He appeared to be seeking a partner who could fill the empty spaces in his life, believing that only then could his life hold meaning. However, he was unaware that he was the gardener of his own life and his life would have meaning once he nurtured his desires and created a fulfilling life with his hands rather than relying on someone else to do it for him.

◻I arrived home to McKenzie playing *Pentatonix* on the radio and wrapping gifts for her friends.

◻"Mum! What happened? You're home so early. Wait, let me guess."

She could see on my face what must have occurred.

◻I took down two plates and served us my hazelnut-encrusted halibut in champagne berry coulis, Israeli couscous, and asparagus with lemon aioli. McKenzie sat savoring the meal.

◻"Well, I fired him. It was a conflict of interest. He was interested, which caused conflict for me. He's so lost, honey. I tried to work with him, but he proved it impossible. It was pitiful to watch."

◻"Mum, he reminds me of the kids you used to work with. You know, the ones you had to teach about being a perfect seed."

◻I nodded in agreement, "You know you're right, honey. He truly believes he was born with a hole in his Soul that can only be filled by someone or something else, not realizing he was born with everything he needed to be something great. It's sad to watch, but ultimately, it is up to him to find himself- to make the changes necessary to see himself in another light."

◻The Director left his job in Boulder and returned to the same town as his ex-wife in Atlanta. I never heard from him again, though I wished him well.

◻Feeling inadequate is a common experience for many people. I recall going through such feelings myself during my first marriage. At that time, I believed that love alone could change my partner. However, I later realized that actual change has to come from within. No matter how much we care for someone, we cannot force them to change. They have to want to change for themselves, and it's essential to recognize and respect their agency in that process.

◻While it can be challenging to see someone we care about struggling and not know how to help, sometimes the best thing we can do is to be there for them and support them in their journey toward growth and self-improvement — but let them walk the walk.

◻We all have encountered someone like the Director, who thinks their life is incomplete without the presence of someone else. However, we were all born with a perfect seed that has the potential to grow and flourish, just like a plant reaching for the Sun. We must embrace our journey, learn from it, and acquire the knowledge required to achieve the life we desire and grow.

Soil Microorganisms

"Microorganisms play a key role in decomposition (the breakdown of organic matter) and the cycling of nutrients and water to our plants and crops. Decaying organic matter provides microorganisms with energy for their growth and supplies carbon for the formation of new cells. As microorganisms help break down organic matter, they release essential nutrients and carbon dioxide into the soil, fix nitrogen, and help transform nutrients into mineral forms that plants can use through a process called mineralization. In addition, as these microorganisms move through the soil, they aerate it, helping to improve soil drainage and soil structure. Because of the role microorganisms play in the environment, the "living soil" is one of the most valuable ecosystems on earth, helping to regulate the climate, mitigate droughts and floods and filter water." ~ *Cedar Circle Farm & Education Center*

Chapter Thirteen

The Garden of Health and Wellness

At 47, I felt healthy and energetic despite having only 60% of my right lung. I stood at 5 foot 3 inches and considered myself in great shape. However, my health soon began to deteriorate.

I started experiencing muscle fatigue while climbing stairs, making it challenging to keep up with my job as a gifted and talented enrichment specialist. I was responsible for training hundreds of teachers in best practices for working with their students. It would take me three weeks to visit all fifteen schools, so the job was challenging, to say the least.

I also noticed that I sometimes struggled to find the right words, making communicating difficult. My usual afternoon three-mile walk became impossible, and I would have to call the Viking King for help, unable to finish my walk and almost in tears.

I wondered if this was the beginning of old age catching up with me. However, my stubbornness refused to accept that possibility, and that trait ultimately saved me.

I was at the top of my career doing what I loved, and my body was failing me.

None of it made sense. I cooked all of my meals from organic sources and watched my portions. Sugar was a treat once a week, so I wasn't overindulging. My sleep was still solid, so why was this happening to me? I was doing everything right to stay vital into my golden years.

Just as a garden needs nourishment and care to grow, the human body also requires sustenance and self-care to develop and thrive. Both the garden and the human body have the potential to flourish when provided with the right conditions, and both can suffer when neglected or exposed to harmful elements.

My body was screaming for help. I was working too hard, stretching myself thin for my job revamping the Gifted and Talented program and training teachers to meet their students' needs. I wanted to give every student a voice, but between juggling 450 students and just as many teachers, I was losing sight of who I was.

When the heart palpitations began, I had no choice but to take three months off from work and eventually leave teaching behind -- feeling deeply conflicted and guilty. My fear of giving up a well-paid career with benefits only added to this stress—a job that had ultimately caused me to get sick.

I strongly cared about my students. However, finding out why my body was revolting against me became my new passion. Little did I know at the time that this would be a journey into understanding how broken our healthcare system is, how the agricultural industry is destroying our food system, and Big Pharma's role in making us sicker.

Life had a funny way of providing the answers. The Viking King and I decided to relocate to Florida and live on a boat. He had dreamed of living on a boat for years after his wife passed, and this seemed to be the right timing and opportunity.

I was also feeling this would be my chance to heal and make sense of what caused my body to give up. I recalled all the times in which doctors had failed me - from my stomach issues as a teenager to the other illnesses I had gone through without receiving a diagnosis or proper treatment.

Living on the boat was a dream, and I started to recuperate from my mysterious illness, though I still couldn't determine the cause apart from extreme exhaustion.

I worked part-time at a jewelry store, lightening some financial pressure. Nonetheless, I still could not put all my energy into something that would not help me advance in life. I dove into my writing after neglecting it for far too long.

Then, in 2017, a casual meeting with an entrepreneur and biohacker would alter the course of my life. The Viking King and I had just sold our boat. We moved into a condominium in Saint Petersburg, Florida. We were not quite ready to return to Boulder, Colorado, and its bitter cold.

During this time, I was writing a screenplay called *Aftermath*. It focused on troubled teenagers with complicated lives who were given the chance to go to the Genesis

Foundation - an institute applying state-of-the-art technology to help these kids become successful members of society on their path to self-improvement.

I interviewed many doctors, scientists, neuroscientists, and researchers creating the latest biotechnology to help assess their patients' health using these transdermal biosensors. I used these tools throughout the film to demonstrate the power of technology and that these integrated medicines are available to those who choose them.

Coincidentally, my new neighbor was The Biohacker, a best-selling author in Australia and a renowned expert in marketing and personal development who had just moved to Florida from New York. He was striving to overcome his fatigue and depression while creating a book that he intended to publish soon. Our first meeting put us on the path to mutually improving our health through biohacking.

The following three years saw me as The Biohacker's copywriter, researching the current health crisis. We interviewed key figures in biohacking while I helped him edit his book; it sold over 60,000 copies within its first year. The online course we developed further enabled over 5,000 people to learn how to increase focus, reduce stress, and eliminate fear.

In addition, the book provided information on nootropics, wearable gadgets, and nutrition for peak performance. It was an ideal union: I got to pursue my passion for writing and medical research while he got to help people take control of their health.

I'd learn how to circumvent our broken healthcare system - by finding specialized doctors in Functional Medicine who helped me recover without any need for dangerous medications - and teach me that there's no one-size-fits-all approach to health. If you google your illness or health concern with the words' functional medicine,' you will see a completely different protocol not utilized by your regular doctor.

Functional medicine doctors were more costly, but I was willing to pay the price for the chance at true wellness. Spending money on supplements and testing seemed more responsible than pouring money towards pharmaceuticals that would never get to the root of my illness.

There were times, however, when I wasn't sure if I would ever be able to make enough progress to live a vibrant life again. Getting my health and vitality back was my new priority.

Just as a garden needs nutrient-rich soil, the human body requires a balanced diet to develop and maintain optimal health. A well-balanced diet gives the body the essential nutrients to function properly, just as nutrient-rich soil provides the garden with the necessary elements to support plant growth. I was eating organic, so why wasn't I getting better?

A farmer must test the soil to see if it is too acidic or if the soil has enough salts, nutrients, and minerals to keep plants healthy.

Testing for these deficiencies became critical to discovering how I could improve my well-being. I used standard lab testing and gold-standard diagnostic tools, such as the DUTCH Complete and the GI Map Test. With these tests, I could finally get a clear picture of what was going on in my body. These tests directly implicated a suffering gut microbiome. I flashed back to my teen years at the nursery and florist shop and realized all of the Round-Up we used to kill the weeds most likely was the culprit in damaging my gut bacteria.

When I was finally diagnosed in 2020 with Hashimotos, an autoimmune disorder, I was determined to restore my health and take control of it. That's when I discovered the value of advanced testing and found dedicated doctors who guided me on this journey. With their help, I could look forward to finding balance in my body again.

As I looked around with this new lens toward medicine, it was hard not to feel a sense of sorrow for so many members of our society who were struggling with their health. The statistics are staggering—Black adults have the highest rate of obesity in America, according to the 2022 State of Obesity report by Trust for America's Health, with 49.9%, compared to 45.6% of Hispanic adults, 41.4% of white adults, and 16.1% of Asian adults. This epidemic is now costing Americans billions of dollars in health care. Yet, we continue to glorify images of unhealthy body types on social media as if it is perfectly normal.

Has anyone asked these people if they knew the root cause of their obesity and if they were willing to find an answer?

I bring up America when discussing our current state of health— we have gone back in time regarding progress. If you compare photos and videos of men and women from the 19th century, they look lithe and fit. Walk yourself into any public gathering place in the twenty-first century, and it's obvious we are suffering from stress, the American diet, and more.

Nowadays, we're facing health epidemics, mental health issues, and a high reliance on prescription drugs. Research has revealed that the European Union restricts genetically modified food sources and chemicals and dyes added to food products; people who visit Europe can testify that the food tastes better. Why has America regressed so much?

◻It's not surprising that two-thirds of American adults are taking prescription drugs, according to Health Policy Institute reports in 2021. It looks like profit is at play in such an alarming statistic.

◻Other countries like Australia and the UK have half the number of people prescribed medication, which leads one to wonder why Americans are so dependent on pills instead of addressing the root causes of their medical issues.

◻With a newfound determination, I launched myself into learning about nutrition and health. I voraciously read labels and chose the most nourishing food options when eating out. I embraced new concepts like tracking macros and strength training for women, ridding my cooking of seed oils, and choosing healthy, natural fats.

◻I found a new love of baking with flour from Europe, which delighted me. I could embrace bread and pasta again without the weight gain and bloat due to our Americanized 'enriched flour.'

◻Where on earth did we think we could do better than Mother Nature? I can picture the discussion with these 'food scientists' in their crazy lab: "Let's create a cheaper flour, pop in a few vitamins, and call it 'enriched.' People will buy it up hook, line, and sinker!'"

◻During the process of enriching our flours, several essential vitamins and minerals such as zinc, magnesium, selenium, and vitamin E are lost along with fiber and protein, while only iron and B vitamins are added back. Grain processing not only destroys vitamins and minerals but also removes natural antioxidants. Unfortunately, these vital nutrients are not added back in, leading to significant nutritional deficiencies in our diets. If you look at most of the population now, 92% of us are dealing with a vitamin deficiency! I knew I just saw the tip of the iceberg, and I was learning so much about our death-and-dying system of health care.

◻Each step brought me closer to discovering my unique approach and what works for me. Despite the occasional detours, I persevered through trial and error until I started seeing results that made me genuinely smile with deep satisfaction at taking back control of my wellbeing.

◻As I delve deeper into my passion for wellness, I have grown to appreciate the importance of giving our bodies what they need and finding simple solutions like returning to nature.

As a child, nature surrounded me with the eleven acres my parents owned for their nursery and florist shop. I spent hours outside with my twin, hiking, fishing, and building forts. I needed to relearn to incorporate the outdoors back into my daily life.

It is crucial to nourish ourselves with water, fresh air, and sunlight as they are fundamental to our wellbeing. Being in nature and soaking up Vitamin D from the Sun does wonders for the body. It's amazing how Mother Nature holds the key to good health.

Nature therapy is a growing trend that should never have gone out of style. Our ancestors were astutely aware of this when they spent most days outside, walking or commuting using horse-drawn buggies. They planted and harvested their own foods, gaining exercise with every calorie burned. Have you ever kneaded your own bread or hung laundry? Those women never had to hit the gym to stay fit and slim because daily activities were enough to keep them healthy.

The beauty of being outdoors allows us to embrace life and our bodies. Oddly, though, once the Viking King and I moved off the boat and back into a house, it was harder for me to get outside except for daily errands and getting mail.

I longed to sit under a tree, listen to the birds, and breathe fresh air. It would take effort to enjoy these simple pleasures, giving me peace and wellness, since I could always make an excuse that I had other things to do.

With our life moving in a new direction again and our eventual move back to Florida, I would make it my next goal to make the outdoors my new sanctuary.

The garden and the human body require regular maintenance to ensure optimal growth and development. In the garden, pruning and weeding help remove dead or diseased plant material and prevent the spread of harmful pests and diseases. Similarly, regular exercise and proper hygiene help remove waste and toxins and prevent the spread of disease.

Through the years of biohacking my health, I learned about detoxing the body from pathogens and toxins and rethinking my water source and where my food came from. I'd rather eat beef from a farmer who loved and cared for his herds than the CAFOs, where thousands of cattle stand in disease-infested paddocks, pumped up on antibiotics, fearfully waiting for slaughter, which causes a heightened cortisol hormone to pump through their organs and muscle- the parts we eat. Cortisol was something I was trying to reduce in my life, so I had to ensure it was out of my food sources.

I also explored the need for supplements during times of stress. The many doctors we interviewed emphasized the importance of various supplements since we no longer get optimal nutrition from our food sources. Selenium, multiple types of magnesium, L-theanine, GABA, Ashwagandha, fish oils, probiotics, and other nootropics were essential in boosting my energy and reducing stress hormones.

￭Although I desperately wished to have my vegetable garden, the limited space left me room for only container gardening. So, I took an alternative approach: shopping at local farmers' markets.

￭I did my best with what America offered and saw noticeable improvements in my strength and physique. However, the next obstacle that lay before me was sleeping.

￭In the same way, a garden needs time to rest before it can grow to rejuvenate its nutrients. My body also required adequate sleep to repair and regenerate itself. Rest and relaxation are essential for maintaining good physical and mental health, just as they are necessary for the growth and development of a garden. I slowly saw this area improve through self-care, taking things slower, meditating, and journaling.

￭We take proper sleep for granted. It was only when my illness made sleeping difficult that I realized how important it was to our physical and mental health. I started researching natural remedies and supplements, such as magnesium oil, melatonin, and L-theanine, to help me get a better and more regular sleep pattern. I had to reduce the cortisol that had overtaken my body. Once the adrenals are chronically stressed, they stay in that stressed mode. Finding ways to reduce the stress response has taken time, but I can now sleep through the night and reset my gut- which has its own circadian rhythm.

A close friend of mine has been caught in a vicious cycle for years due to a demanding work schedule. He has always considered himself a night owl. However, he is now retired and continues to go to bed in the early morning, not waking until noon, and is suffering from several chronic health issues. Our bodies need to follow a natural sleep pattern aligned with the Sun. Years of sleep deprivation have altered his gut bacteria, which increases the risk of developing various metabolic and inflammatory diseases like obesity, diabetes, inflammatory bowel diseases, and asthma. He suffers from several of these disorders but doesn't want to take his lifestyle into consideration.

It's becoming increasingly clear that paying attention to our diet and lifestyle can help heal our gut microbiome for better health.

￭I also made some lifestyle changes that positively impacted my sleeping habits. I cut back on caffeine, took cortisol management supplements, adopted a consistent bedtime routine that included writing in my journal or reading something calming before bed, and eliminated all screens -phones, TVs, etc.- close to an hour before bedtime. I concentrated on balancing my hormones and took supplements for any deficiencies that impacted my quality of sleep.

I also noticed that spending the morning hours on our porch, watching the sunrise, reset my circadian rhythm, so sleep came more naturally. There is so much to say about our need for natural sunlight that a vitamin D supplement cannot replicate.

These practices were very effective in helping me fall asleep faster and stay asleep through the night. By making these changes, I could experience restful nights of deep sleep with no disturbances, which gave me the energy I needed during the day.

I started practicing yoga again, which improved my balance and flexibility and helped me relax my mind and body, improving my sleep quality. Along with yoga, I went back to meditation, which reduced stress.

Overall, making simple changes in my lifestyle helped tremendously in improving my physical and mental health over time.

Experiencing eight years of ill health and recovery taught me the importance of health and wellbeing for making the most out of life in our later years.

I advise anyone to find a doctor specializing in Functional medicine. These doctors not only have a Ph.D. from medical school but have further educated themselves on how all body systems work together to get to the root of the matter and find healing protocols for their patients. They typically spend about 40 minutes or more with a patient at a time to go over extensive questions for each system of the body, including nutrition.

It is not a well-known fact that only one-quarter of medical schools offer a nutrition course as an elective, and most of those courses last only a week if the medical student chooses that elective. More time is needed to grasp how diet and lifestyle deeply influence human physiology.

Medical students must be further trained to understand nutrition's impact on the body and to find correlations between nutrition and disease.

Functional medicine doctors also use state-of-the-art testing to identify the root cause of diseases. It was only through this testing that I discovered my autoimmune issue, which was affecting my thyroid. I could elaborate on how our general doctors do not utilize complete thyroid testing protocols, which include eight markers to test for. They typically only test for TSH and maybe one other marker, which provides a skewed picture of what is really going on with our thyroid. An estimated 20 million Americans have some form of thyroid disease. **Up to 60 percent** of those with thyroid disease are unaware of their condition. Thanks to the comprehensive testing, my doctor was well-informed about how to treat my illness and provided me with the proper protocol to follow.per protocol to follow.

Since my body demonstrated to me at a young age not to take it for granted with my collapsed lung, I now realize our health and wellbeing are all we have in this life that we can control- for the most part. I want to dance into my nineties with the vibrancy allowed to us, and I want that for you, too.

I believe that everyone deserves to live a healthy and fulfilling life, and I'm confident that my carefully curated resources can help you achieve just that. During my time as a research writer, I have interviewed hundreds of doctors, scientists, and experts who helped me put together a comprehensive collection of tools and information to guide you on your journey to health and wellness. Whether you're looking to improve your health or overall well-being,

Garden of Eden

The Garden of Eden represents a region of Being in which all primal ideas for the production of the beautiful. As described in Genesis, it represents, allegorically, the elemental life and intelligence placed at the disposal of man and through which he is to evolve both mind and body.

CHAPTER FOURTEEN

How to Create Your Garden of Eden From The Compost Heap You Created

In the garden of life, composting represents the ability to take what may seem like waste or setbacks and turn them into something valuable and beneficial. Just as composting requires a mix of different organic materials to create a balanced and nutrient-rich soil amendment, you can combine your own experiences, both positive and negative, to cultivate personal growth and resilience.

I went through this process when I turned 33 years old. I knew my marriage was over. I was trying to find the right path to take with my daughter that would leave the least amount of scars. I didn't want to rush into such an enormous decision since it involved uprooting the only life McKenzie knew. She was only eleven, yet I had planned to free ourselves from the cloud hanging over us for years.

I had to turn over the soil of the past twenty years with Jack, reliving the times of abuse and trauma. Where was my part in the equation? I couldn't just blame everything on him and his behavior. This one step of realization — a huge step — helped me gain the perspective I needed to start walking on this new journey of self-discovery and responsibility for my choices.

How many times have we seen someone we care about keep making the same mistakes over and over again? Their compost heap grew because they feared confronting all they attributed to their hardships. It takes a lot of courage to face this pile of manure and begin digging at it, one issue at a time.

I could have ignored the havoc I lived in and left my pile of dung alone. But I became keenly aware that I wanted this lifetime to count. I did not want to repeat these painful lessons if I believed in Earth being our life school. So, I began breaking the ground, pulling out the weeds, and finding the rocks I had buried deep within. This process took on many forms.

The first step to creating something new in your life is to sift through the manure you've dealt with over the years and examine the material closely to see where you contributed.

These gathered materials of misgivings and tribulations must be adequately mixed and regularly turned into a compost pile. This process allows for proper aeration and decomposition. In life, we must actively engage with our experiences, reflecting on them regularly and seeking ways to learn and grow from them. This continuous self-reflection and personal development process is like turning the compost pile.

This process is akin to a seed buried in the soil, ensuring all the necessary elements and conditions are present for it to sprout and grow. Just as the seed prefers to be in darkness during this process, we also seek solitude for introspection, needing to be alone to reflect and process. I reflected on my experiences and identified the lessons I learned from each challenging situation. I had to face where I was at fault or where I may have contributed to the issues. These lessons serve as the foundation for personal growth and development. I did the work through journaling or talking with a counselor or trusted friend.

Some close to me asked how anything I did as a child contributed to the situation. Yes, children should be exempt from facing the traumas given to them by older perpetrators; however, what if my lesson was to speak up until I was heard? If I had gone to the school counselor or spoken to other family and friends, if I felt worthy of being respected, then that may have settled the matter directly, and my sister would not have been able to get away with what she did.

But I recall feeling stuck. I was stuck with parents who didn't see the travesty of allowing a child to dictate how the family should live. I saw this repeat in my life when I felt powerless, but it was more of me feeling not worthy of protection. Regardless of the actual name of my false perceptions, I knew I had to be the one to change.

Journaling became the most powerful tool. It was like reaching into the ether; answers would come to all the questions I wrote down. My intuition grew, and I could sense the answers to my questions unfolding on the pages, guiding me along the way. I felt lighter and calmer each time I journaled my thoughts, fears, and desires.

Whenever I feel lost, I pick up my journal and ask the Universe to supply the answers. Over the years, this has evolved to just sitting quietly for an extended period and observing the waves of energy around me. I ask a question and sit with it. If I'm calm enough, a whisper of thought will come to me—much like the journal.

I often reflect on how much I grew during my first marriage with Jack. I realized I deserved a better life when I stood up for myself. However, our relationship didn't change until I realized that I was the one who needed to change first.

I was growing, and Jack was not. I faced each turmoil with determination not to get emotionally charged anymore. I began to witness his fear and did not allow it to trigger mine.

His aggression stemmed from a deep-seated desire to evoke a similar response from me, perpetuating a cycle of pain. However, I made the conscious choice to maintain inner peace. This marked the beginning of our disconnection. I came to understand that he was a man in pain, seeking to engage with another person in pain. By refusing to let his aggression affect me, I stripped him of his power over me.

It's similar to when a prey turns on its predator—unexpectedly, the predator lets go! Jack wasn't able to rile me up. I stopped trying to negotiate with him to stay home with McKenzie and me and not go to the Sports Book. I no longer waited for him to invite us to join him, and I started doing things that McKenzie and I would find joyful.

Jack's anger no longer affected me, and I was finally free.

As time passes, microorganisms break down the organic matter in the compost pile, transforming it into nutrient-rich humus. Similarly, through introspection, you can transform your challenges into valuable lessons that nourish your personal development. These lessons become the fertile soil where beautiful gardens of resilience, wisdom, and strength can grow.

This time in my life was full of reading books. I read as much as possible about self-growth, resilience, and life lessons. I delved into the world of Spiritual awareness, working on my intuition and building confidence in my ability to discern the people around me. I practiced my intuitive abilities on Facebook groups, growing in confidence each time I read someone accurately.

I wasn't afraid to look closely at my mistakes and see each as a lesson I needed to learn. I also found that a new test would emerge to see if I could apply my new knowledge to new situations. Each new test helped build my confidence and understanding of why I needed to learn the lesson. Self-worth, self-reliance, and self-love were the lessons I honed; if I forgot, it would come again to help me practice what I wasn't understanding.

This came through another relationship with a man who helped me hone my intuition since I wasn't relying on my gut instinct as I should.

I met this man I will call Anthony. Unlike my ex-husband, Anthony had a way with words, so our conversations never ceased. He traveled often and told stories of incredible restaurants and places he visited. I was intrigued.

Anthony became my confidant, having helped another woman get out of an abusive relationship. I relied on his counsel, knowing I might need someone to help me and McKenzie leave should Jack become violent with our impending divorce.

Anthony watched over us from afar. He respected my marriage, though he wanted McKenzie and me to be safe, and offered us protection if needed. Anthony had another life, however. He commuted between Boulder and Los Angeles, coming home on the weekends.

Many months after my divorce was finalized, our friendship turned into romance -though it was hard to navigate. Anthony wouldn't quite commit to us, often teasing how he preferred the mystique of an Asian woman, and I was far from those dark-haired beauties.

I began noticing inklings of my gut instinct toward Anthony's behavior. He carried his cell phone on his hip, never allowing it to sit in easy view. He would text me sensual innuendos, and I realized how easy it would be for him to have other intimate encounters with other women on his phone.

My instincts heightened, and my gut told me he wasn't being faithful. It would take a chance moment when a nurse handed Anthony's personal belongings to me during his shoulder surgery; I would find out the truth: he had five Asian beauties at his beck and call. This is for another story.

I left him, never looking back. I learned much about trusting your gut and not depending on having hard evidence to back up your feelings.

I felt liberated. I finally had the tools to help navigate the complexities of relationships. That is when I met my husband, a man of integrity, loyalty, great humor, and love. After all my deep self-examination and personal development efforts, I could now enjoy the fruits of my labor.

One way to identify unresolved issues is to share your story with someone and notice if you are still experiencing the same emotions as if it happened yesterday. If the feelings cause your heart to pound, your breathing to heighten, or your voice to become sharp, then more work must be done to heal these unresolved emotions. Only after there is no emotion left in the story will wisdom remain. Ben was a perfect example of this test. Even after ten years, he had unresolved issues with his divorce.

By reading my stories, I hope you can see there isn't a magic pill or a costly course to follow. It is an ever-evolving process you must follow to become the person you are meant to be. I have assembled an easy step-by-step process to walk you through any issue you want to overcome.

Step 1: Acknowledgment and Acceptance

The first step in coming to terms with issues in my life was acknowledging and accepting them as part of my personal experience. This involved recognizing negative emotions, such as anger, sadness, or fear, and allowing myself to feel them fully. I needed to understand that these emotions are natural responses to challenging situations, not signs of weakness. This acknowledgment and acceptance paved the way for further self-reflection and growth, enabling me to address and work through my emotions in a healthy manner. Ultimately, this led to a sense of empowerment and resilience.

I was lucky not to balk at looking closely at myself. However, my mother refused to see her part in our trauma. Maybe it was instinctual, but I refused to be so close-minded. I know I am here to learn; failure is the best teacher.

An influential book that helped guide me during this time was Eckhart Tolle's "A New Earth." In this book, he explains the concept of the "pain body," which is the collection of negative emotional pain and thought patterns that individuals carry throughout their lives. The pain body can be triggered by various events, conversations, and thoughts, and it can manifest in different forms such as hurt, hate, depression, self-hate, anxiety, fear, alienation, despair, emotional drama, blame, and even physical illness. It can be either active or dormant, and it has the potential to take over the mind. For it to thrive, it must feed off someone else's "pain body," giving it more reason to thrive.

After learning about this, I realized that I was reacting to my ex-husband's "pain body" and anger. Once I stopped feeding into his emotional turmoil, I was able to disconnect from him without any further emotional trauma safely. It's important to note, however, that Tolle explains once you can achieve this, the other person's reaction to you being able to ignore their behavior may cause a heightened threat in their mind. They may become more aggressive or angered since they can no longer engage your "pain body."

Step 2: Reflection and Self-Examination

The second step for me was reflection and self-examination. I found it helpful to carefully analyze the situations, identify the root causes of the issues, and consider how they had impacted my life. I often took the time to write down my thoughts and feelings in a journal, which helped me gain clarity. Discussing these thoughts with a trusted friend or therapist can also be beneficial. This process has led to new insights and a deeper understanding of myself, which I find incredibly valuable.

I read Janet Connor's book Writing Down Your Soul: How to Activate and Listen to the Extraordinary Voice Within, where I found the connection to my intuition. I would get little whispers and sensations of a new thought and write it down after asking a question. I was sometimes surprised by the answers since I disagreed with some of them, but ultimately, I knew they were right, and it was most likely my ego getting involved. I highly suggest looking into automatic writing to get closer to your innate introspections.

Step 3: Forgiveness and Letting Go

The third step is forgiveness and letting go. It is often misunderstood and carries a negative belief, suggesting the other person should be "let off the hook," so to speak. However, the step of forgiveness or letting go may involve forgiving oneself for past mistakes or regrets and forgiving others who have caused harm or hurt feelings, so you are not holding onto anger or resentment. Carrying a grudge only serves to perpetuate negative emotions and hinder personal growth, as well as affecting our physical health. Practicing forgiveness can lead to greater peace of mind and improved relationships with others.

Step 4: Learning from Past Experiences

The fourth step is learning from past experiences by recognizing the lessons that can be gained from difficult situations and applying them to future experiences. It can be helpful to identify specific skills or knowledge that can be developed to prevent similar issues from arising again. Such skills could be problem-solving, effective communication, time management, and conflict resolution. All of us could do a little refresher course on personality traits and the psychology of relationships.

Step 5: Taking Action

The final step is addressing the underlying causes of the issues and making positive changes in one's life. This may involve setting goals, developing new habits, seeking resources or support, or making necessary adjustments in relationships or work situations. Taking action demonstrates a commitment to personal growth and can lead to greater satisfaction and fulfillment in life.

These steps have helped me make significant changes by setting boundaries with the people around me. I've learned to hold myself to a higher standard when choosing whom to trust and be friends with. This has dramatically improved my life, and I strive to influence others as well positively. Your lessons may differ vastly, but the process is the same. It takes a person of emotional intelligence to recognize the changes they need to make.

Just as the compost has matured into a rich humus, it can nourish plants in the garden. I could apply my newfound wisdom and resilience to various aspects of my life, such as relationships, career, and personal goals. This nourishment allowed the growth of beautiful gardens filled with happiness, success, and fulfillment.

CHAPTER FIFTEEN

The Gardener's Guide to Life

The tradition of setting New Year's resolutions is common across many cultures. It's a time when we reflect on the past year and look forward to the possibilities of the new one. However, more often than not, we find ourselves needing help to keep up with the goals we set for ourselves. The feeling of defeat can be overwhelming, leading to a sense of hopelessness as we enter the new year. Despite this, it's important to remember that change is a process that takes time and effort. However, we can look to Mother Nature to help create a path towards success and find motivation to keep moving forward.

As human beings, we all have a strong desire for change and growth. However, creating and maintaining new habits can be a difficult task. It is known in academic circles that it takes at least three weeks to form a new habit, but what if we could use the natural rhythm of the seasons to guide us in creating lasting change? Each season lasts three months, giving us a perfect timeframe to establish and stick to new habits. Using the changing seasons as a framework for personal growth, we can develop a sense of consistency and purpose in our lives. So, let's look to the seasons for guidance and inspiration to create positive and lasting change in our lives.

Navigating Life's Journey Through the Seasons

The seasons can serve as a guide when it comes to health, wellness, and self-development. Each season brings unique characteristics and qualities that can be harnessed to support our well-being and personal growth. By aligning ourselves with the natural rhythms of the seasons, we can optimize our physical, mental, and emotional health.

Too often, we feel compelled to start the New Year with resolutions that, when unresolved, create guilt and resentment. We begin again, only feeling overwhelmed and let down. That is why Mother Nature is the best guide. Nature respects the cycles. There is a balance that respects the time to mate or to feed or not to feed. Our conscious and analytical mind gets in the way of this balance.

Spring

Spring is a season of renewal and growth. It symbolizes new beginnings, fresh starts, and the awakening of nature after the dormant winter period. Concerning our health and wellness, Spring is an ideal time for detoxification and cleansing. Just as nature sheds its old layers, we can also let go of toxins accumulated in our bodies through cleansing practices such as fasting or adopting a cleaner diet.

Spring is a great time to declutter the closets and drawers. We all have that one area in our home we would rather not go to since it feels overwhelming to fix. Remember my students and how they learned to be mindful with every task. Sure, there are days you want to walk away from something, but if you decide to apply mindfulness to these activities, I'll guarantee they will get done, and you'll feel much better. Listening to a podcast or music can also be a great way to pass the time.

Spring is also a great time to engage in physical activities that promote flexibility and mobility, such as yoga or tai chi. Spring encourages you to move like a good stretch when getting out of bed after a long sleep. Emotionally, Spring encourages us to embrace change and explore new possibilities. It is a time to set goals, plan, and take action towards personal growth.

Summer

Summer represents warmth, energy, and abundance. It is a season of vitality and activity. During this time, we can focus on nourishing our bodies with fresh fruits and vegetables that are abundant in this season. Eating colorful foods rich in vitamins and minerals can support our immune system and overall well-being.

Summer is also an excellent time for outdoor activities like swimming, hiking, or cycling, providing physical exercise and sunlight exposure for vitamin D synthesis. Emotionally, summer invites us to embrace joy, playfulness, and creativity. It is a time to engage in hobbies or activities that bring pleasure and allow us to express ourselves fully.

Autumn

Autumn signifies change, transition, and harvest. As the leaves change color and fall from the trees, autumn reminds us of the impermanence of life. It is a season for reflection, letting go, and preparing for the colder months. In terms of health and wellness, this is a time to strengthen our immune system in preparation for the colder months ahead. We can focus on consuming warming foods like soups, stews, and herbal teas that support our digestion and provide nourishment. Learning to cook the season's rich foods also helps us engage more closely with nature.

Autumn is also an ideal time for introspection and self-reflection. It encourages us to evaluate our goals, assess our progress, and make any necessary adjustments. Emotionally, autumn invites us to practice gratitude and embrace change with acceptance and resilience.

Winter

Winter represents stillness, rest, and introspection. It is a season of hibernation and conservation of energy. During winter, it is crucial to prioritize self-care and nourishment. This includes getting enough sleep, maintaining a balanced diet, and engaging in activities that promote relaxation and stress reduction, such as meditation or gentle yoga.

Winter is also an excellent time for learning and self-development. With more indoor time available, we can focus on reading books, taking online courses, or engaging in creative pursuits that stimulate our minds. Emotionally, winter encourages us to cultivate patience, resilience, and inner strength. It is a time for self-reflection, introspection, and setting intentions for the upcoming year.

The seasons can serve as a guide for health and wellness by providing us with cues on aligning ourselves with nature's natural rhythms. By embracing the qualities of each season and adapting our lifestyle accordingly, we can optimize our physical well-being, nurture our emotional health, and foster personal growth.

***

Seasonal Journaling: A Guide to Reflecting and Growing Throughout the Year

Each season brings questions about our progress or lack thereof in life. Nature carries that balance that we all strive for, and there is a process that creates this balance. When you look at your life like a garden, you can ask yourself the questions that may be eluding you. Below are the guidelines for growing a beautiful Eden in your life.

Ask yourself these prompts in a journal throughout the year. You may come to some realizations or insights that help you dig a little deeper into an essential aspect of your life, or you may have neglected to reflect on a factor altogether.

Nurture your roots:

Just like a plant needs strong roots to grow and thrive, so do we need a strong foundation of self-care and self-love to live a quality life. This includes caring for our physical, emotional, and mental health and cultivating positive relationships with others.

What are some ways you can nurture your roots and build a strong foundation of self-care and self-love?
What are some changes you can make for your physical body?
How is your mental health and relationships working for you?

Tend to your soil:

The soil in a garden provides nutrients and support for the plants to grow. Similarly, we must nurture our inner resources and support systems to live a quality life. This includes developing a growth mindset, practicing gratitude, and seeking mentors and role models.

What are some ways in which you can nurture your inner resources and support systems to live a quality life?

Share some gratitude in your journal each day to change the filter you see in life.

Are the people you surround yourself with the people you want to become?

Water wisely:

Overwatering can be just as harmful as underwatering a garden. Similarly, we need to be mindful of allocating our time, energy, and resources to avoid burnout and maintain a healthy life balance.

How have you been allotting your time?
Where in your life seems out of balance?
How do you reset yourself from the digital and technological world?

Prune with intention:

Pruning a garden helps to promote healthy growth and remove dead or damaged branches. Likewise, we must intentionally set boundaries, let go of negative influences, and cultivate a sense of purpose and direction.

Where do you need to set boundaries?
Are there any negative influences in your life?
How are you cultivating purpose in your life?

Bask in the Sun:

Sunlight is essential for plant growth, and it can also have a profound impact on our well-being. Spending time in nature, getting enough sleep, and practicing mindfulness can all help to improve our physical and mental health.

In what ways are you adding the Sun into your life through nature, sleep, and mindfulness? Do you need more?

What part of your life do you need to embrace? This could be a challenge you are currently facing, and you may need to change your perspective about it.

Embrace the seasons:

A garden experiences different seasons throughout the year, each with unique challenges and opportunities, so we must be adaptable and open to change, embracing each season as a chance for growth and renewal.

Where are you resisting change in your life?

Cultivate diversity:

A diverse garden is more resilient and vibrant, with a greater variety of plants and animals. We must cultivate diversity in our lives, seeking different perspectives, experiences, and connections to enrich our lives and broaden our horizons.

How are you adding diversity to your life?
Where is diversity lacking?
Is there a situation you could change your perspective on that would make a positive change for yourself?

Let go of perfection:

No garden is perfect, and neither are we. We must let go of the idea of perfection and embrace the beauty of imperfection, accepting ourselves and others just as we are.

In what areas in your life are you hard on yourself?

How can you improve your perspective?

In what ways can you embrace this aspect of yourself or change it?

Nurture your sense of wonder:

A garden can be a source of endless wonder and awe, full of surprises and discoveries. We must nurture our sense of wonder and curiosity, seeking new experiences and perspectives to keep our lives fresh and exciting.

Have you been holding back from new experiences? Why?

List five new things you'd like to experience.

Celebrate the harvest:

A garden's bounty is a source of joy and celebration, a reminder of the hard work and dedication to its cultivation. We must celebrate our achievements and blessings, no matter how small they seem.

Write all of the things that are going right in your life! Express the little achievements you've been working on. Here is where you toot your own horn!

***

Below are prompts to help you reset and reconfigure your mindset during each change of the Seasons. You will continue with the prompts above but then incorporate the seasonal questions since each part of the year brings about a nuance of change. Just as the animals prepare for each season, you must look ahead to what you want your life to look like and how you'd like to grow.

Spring Journal Questions

1. What type of detoxification and cleansing practices do you plan to incorporate into your routine for the spring season?

2. How are you approaching decluttering and organizing your living space this Spring?

3. How are you integrating mindfulness into daily tasks and activities?

4. In what ways have you been embracing physical activities?

5. What are three goals you are setting for personal growth?

Summer Journal Questions

1. How are you incorporating a summer diet to boost your immune system? Which foods should you rethink in your diet?

2. How could you improve your knowledge about the proper diet for you?

3. How do you intend to increase your outdoor physical activity during the summer months?

4. What specific hobby or activity do you plan to engage in to embrace joy and creativity this summer?

5. How do you plan to ensure you are getting enough sunlight exposure for vitamin D synthesis during the summer?

Autumn Journal Questions

1. What warming foods can you incorporate into your diet to support your immune system during the colder months?

2. How can you engage more closely with nature through cooking the season's rich foods?

3. How can you practice gratitude and embrace change with acceptance and resilience during the autumn season?

4. How can you incorporate self-reflection and introspection into your daily routine during autumn?

5. What steps can you take to evaluate your goals, assess your progress, and make any necessary adjustments during this season of change?

Winter Journal Questions

1. What are some activities you plan to do to incorporate rest and relaxation?

2. How do you plan to prioritize self-care during the winter and holiday season?

3. What books or online courses do you plan to engage with during the winter months?

4. What creative pursuits or hobbies do you want to explore during the winter?

5. What are your intentions or goals for personal growth and development during this winter?

6. How do you plan to incorporate balance when it comes to the holidays?

This guide to life offers many valuable lessons for living a quality life. By living purposefully and tending to our own needs, we can grow and thrive in our lives, just like a beautiful garden.

<h1 style="text-align:center">About the Author</h1>

Deborah Holmén is a seasoned writer and author who focuses on personal growth and writes books and articles on mental health and wellness. With over 25 years of experience as a National Board Certified Teacher with a Masters in Teacher Leadership, Deborah brings a unique perspective on the human experience and relationships. Her content covers a wide range of topics, from relationships and parenting to personal development, and is designed to help individuals lead happier and healthier lives. Her first book, *The Biohacker's Guide to Keto & Fasting for Women Over 40: Rediscover Your Body's Intuition on What and When to Eat, was* published in 2018. Deborah's writing can be found in various publications like The Goodman Project, Change Becomes You, A Parent is Born, Illumination, Medium, and more.

Over the years, Deborah has explored the intersection of health and wellness and used her writing skills to help others heal. She has worked as a ghostwriter for the health and wellness industry and has helped shed light on various mental health and wellness topics. As a result of her work, she has developed a deep understanding of the most effective techniques for promoting mental health and wellness. She draws on this experience to create content that is informative, useful, and actionable.

Deborah has included various QR codes for readers to check out throughout the book, providing easily accessible information she mentions. If you've never used a QR code before [the fancy squares at the end of the chapters],

point your phone camera at the image. A yellow Chrome link will appear. Do not take a photo. Just tap the yellow link, and it will take you to the appropriate page.

Please contact Deborah Holmen at deborah@deborahholmen.com should you find a link that no longer works or for any other reason.

Since links take readers to Deborah's Amazon storefront, Deborah will receive a tiny commission if readers click on the affiliates/advertisers' links and make a purchase. Deborah advertises products she believes in and has personally tried or utilized in her twenty-five years in academia and as a writer in the health and wellness industry.

Acknowledgements

We meet so many people on our journey when delving into our passions. It could be the teacher or professor who told you you had it in you to do great things or the stranger who listened to your story on a plane and wanted to hear more. Those people go without a name but are just as important as those I am honored to call friend, colleague, daughter and husband.

To Mother Nature and the infinite wisdom and lessons you teach us every day. Thank you!

To my family, who were my first teachers on this life journey. Without you, I wouldn't be the woman I am today. I love you.

To my daughter, who is a part of many of the stories still shaping the woman you call Mum. Without your belief in me as a writer, I wouldn't be writing this acknowledgment. You inspire me every day to be a better woman and mother.

To my students! You never knew how much you all meant to me each passing year, but each of you inspired me to be a better teacher. You taught me so much about the human condition, and I love all of you for allowing me to 'experiment' with you on what makes you, you!

To the Viking King, you were the one who showed me I finally deserve a great and lasting love with plenty of laughs, deep respect, and adventures. My work is becoming a reality because of your persistence and undying support!

For Leanne and Ms. Leaf, my friends who have always had my back and supported me! I love you!